THE BELL AND THE DRUM

The Bell and the Drum

SHIH CHING AS FORMULAIC POETRY IN AN ORAL TRADITION

C. H. Wang

UNIVERSITY OF CALIFORNIA PRESS

Berkeley, Los Angeles, London

University of California Press
Berkeley and Los Angeles, California
University of California Press, Ltd.
London, England
Copyright © 1974, by
The Regents of the University of California
ISBN: 0–520–02441–9
Library of Congress Catalog Card Number: 73–76104
Printed in the United States of America

To the Memory of
CHEN SHIH-HSIANG
(1912–1971)

CONTENTS

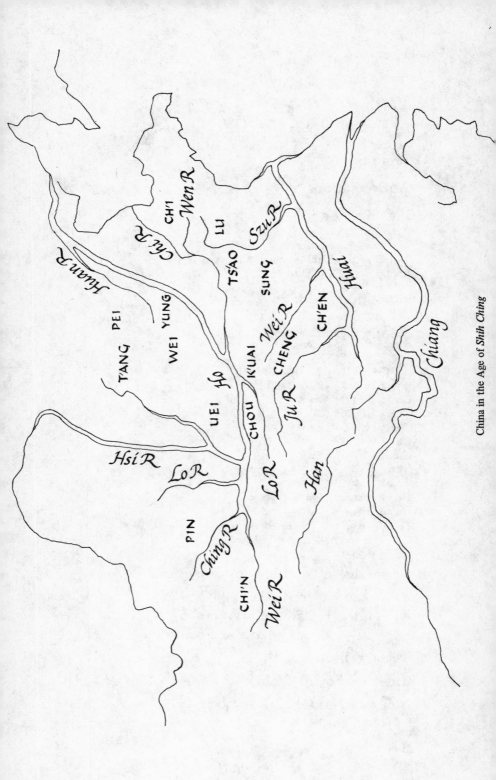

China in the Age of *Shih Ching*

PREFACE

When the poet finishes his *Kuan chü* in praise of a girl by mentioning the bell and the drum, whose music delights her heart, he does not present her a manuscript, but a song. The last line of *Kuan chü* involves naïveté (in the sense used by Friedrich Schiller), for it is the line, buoyant and resounding, that betrays the mechanism of the poem, the mechanism of *Kuan chü* and of all other early Chinese poems. The poet sings, in accord with the pitch, tone, and rhythm produced by various musical instruments; the bell and the drum are used mainly in the case of *Shih Ching*.

Confucius heard the poem of *Kuan chü*, among others similar in type and value, sung by some music master in the sixth century B.C., and exclaimed: "How magnificently it filled the ears!" By then, the poem had been transmitted and probably polished and modified by the professional singer, the music master. By then, other instruments than just the bell and the drum were probably used in the performance. In Confucius' time the poetry of ancient China, including *Kuan chü*, was taking its final, definite shape; its prototypal form, of great diversity and unity, was becoming for the Chinese in the following millennia the form of *Shih Ching*. The form of *Shih Ching* was the only basic form of *shih*, or poetry; and the content, which the form defines, embodies some of the most trenchant and surging themes to recur and vary throughout the Chinese poetic tradition. Recognizing that the poetic mechanism is qualified by the musical instruments, I attempt in this book to describe the form of *Shih Ching* by manifesting its mode of imaginative creation in an age of oral composition, and to identify some primary poetic conventions, in order to read the poetry of ancient China as it was heard by the girl of *Kuan chü* and by others in similar cultural circumstances.

By form, I refer to a discernible acoustic pattern which, in *Shih Ching*, is both dynamic and organic. The acoustic pattern is organic because it is determined essentially by the cadential unit of the bell and the drum, and other instruments. The cadential unit, of a variety of types, proliferates and multiplies to constitute the pattern. The cadential unit, while in deference to a *nómos*, is demonstrably protean, for it is the reflection of the poet's free operation of mind and imagination at a time when poetry, by definition, rejects prosodic stricture. On the other hand, the acoustic pattern is dynamic because it not only admits but invites stock phrases (which are called "formulas" in the present study) and type-scenes (which are called "themes") to achieve the totality of associations which the poet and his audience seek. The dynamic nature of the pattern is evident also in that the formulas are fluid and mobile: they contract, expand, and generate and define one another; and that the themes are now rigid and now flexible in the imagistic concatenation. The problem of form and its relation to content has entered the consideration of some traditional and modern students of *Shih Ching*. With few exceptions, however, they stop at the inspection of prosodic principles and rhetorical devices, thinking that these are the only legitimate components of the poetic form. In order to have the naïveté regained, I propose to investigate the *Shih Ching* poetry by constantly referring to its acoustic pattern, which I take to be the true meaning of *form*. By emphasizing the acoustic pattern in broad terms, instead of the metapoetic rules and findings, I am reiterating the theory that the poetry of *Shih Ching* has an oral origin. It is conceivably oral, and demonstrably formulaic. In view of the oral-formulaic nature of *Shih Ching*, I have joined with other Parryists in the fields of literary studies to demand a new method of analysis and a new criterion of evaluation in dealing with poetry of that particular nature; and I believe that, with this new attitude toward the classics, we will attain a new delight in the reading of naive poetry.

The approach is, therefore, generally comparative. For the affirmation of a comparative approach to classical Chinese poetry, I am thankful to many scholars at the University of California, Berkeley, for their encouragement. To Professors Cyril Birch, Alain Renoir, Michael N. Nagler, Joseph Duggan, and the late Professor Peter A. Boodberg I am indebted for their advice, help, and suggestions in the reading and criticism of the Greek, Old English, and Chinese documents prior to and during the writing of my doctoral dissertation, out of which this book has evolved. To the late Professor Chen Shih-hsiang, my debt is beyond expression. It was he who equipped me with an unfailing love for the Chinese classics and the courage to be in and out of them to confront a modern Chinese mentality which sometimes questions their value and even tries to deprive them of the right to continue to exist. I dedicate this book to him, in memory, with gratitude for his inspiration of that love and courage.

To Professors C. T. Hsia, Earl Miner, Frederic Will, Warren D. Anderson, and Robert P. Creed, I owe many valuable suggestions for the improvement of the organization and style of this book at various stages. I also want to express my deep appreciation to Professors Chow Tse-tsung, Hsü Fu-kuan, and Paul L-M Serruys for their piercing, stimulating comments, which often forced me to reconsider important issues in the formulaic analysis of an ancient Chinese poem. I have a debt of gratitude to Professor Frederick W. Mote for his perceptive and thoughtful comments on the manuscript at the last minute, and his interpretation that in examining the process of the making of a *Shih Ching* poem one reflects on the problem of the making of history, as if also by formulas and themes.

ABBREVIATIONS

Feng   *Kuo feng* 國風
H. Ya   *Hsiao ya* 小雅
T. Ya   *Ta ya* 大雅
Chou S.   *Chou sung* 周頌
Lu S.   *Lu sung* 魯頌
Shang S.   *Shang sung* 商頌

BIHP   *Bulletin of the Institute of History and Philology,* Academia
   Sinica 中央研究院歷史語言研究所集刊
SPPY   *Szu-pu pei-yao* 四部備要
SPTK   *Szu-pu ts'ung-k'an* 四部叢刊
SSCCS   *Shih-san-ching chu shu* 十三經注疏
THHP   *Ts'ing-hua hsüeh-pao* 清華學報
YCHP   *Yen-ching hsüeh-pao* 燕京學報

AJP   *American Journal of Philology*
ELH   *English Literary History*
HSCP   *Harvard Studies in Classical Philology*
MP   *Modern Philology*
PMLA   *Publications of the Modern Languages Association*
PQ   *Philological Quarterly*
TPAPA   *Transactions and Proceedings of the American Philological Asso-
   ciation*
UCPCP   *University of California Publications in Classical Philology*

ONE

Introduction

FROM SONG TO POEM

In the study of Chinese literature, traditional critics and historians have directed more attention to speculation on theme than to the apprehension of form. This tendency is also true in *Shih Ching* (詩經) scholarship. The thematic speculation of some critics, moreover, aims at allegorization, a bent which often bypasses the aesthetic aspect of what we now call literature. To begin with, the "Great Preface" (大序) of *Shih Ching* stresses exactly that the function of poetry is to be beneficial rather than to delight.[1] When *prodesse* is more important than *delectare,* to confirm an allegory of ethics in the poem certainly appears to a student more pressing and consequential than to appreciate its literal meaning. The formative trope which determines a poem's aesthetic value, therefore, seldom enters his consideration.

The susceptibility to allegorization in the traditional *Shih Ching* scholarship is a manifest distortion of this classic anthology, a distortion both of its genetic character and of the original definition of *shih* in general. That the *Shih Ching* lyrics originated in music is unquestionable. While in *Shang Shu* (尚書) *shih* and *ko* (歌) are mentioned together and are almost interchangeable in their denotations, the principal description that follows the epithet is absolutely unrelated to ethics. The elements of form occupy the earliest account of poetry in Chinese letters:

[1]先王以是經夫婦，成孝敬，厚人倫，美教化，移風俗 (With it, the earlier kings regulated the married couple, established the principle of filial piety, intensified human relationships, elevated civilization, and improved the public morals.)

I

詩言志，歌永言；聲依永，律和聲。八音克諧無相奪，
神人以和。[2]

Poetry verbalizes intents; song intones the verbalization;
notes comply with the intonation; and musical rules
regulate the notes. The eight sounds are accordant, not to
interfere with one another; spirits and men are thereby
in harmony.

At this stage, achieving harmony between man and nature and
moving even the beasts to dancing, as the subsequent passages in
Shang Shu indicate, are the true functions of poetry.[3] *Delectare* is
more essential than *prodesse*. Cheng Hsüan (鄭玄) recognizes this
as probably the primordial character of Chinese poetry, and he
tries to link the poetry of *Shih Ching* with it.[4] However, as one of
the most accomplished allegorists in the history of the *Shih Ching*
commentary, Cheng, on the other hand, dissociates *shih* from the
ko tradition and instead brings the former into relation with *li* (禮),
or ritual propriety, in order to suit his allegorizing attitude. He
assumes that in the beginning, when poetry was also song, it was
straightforward and hence plain, and earnestness was its principle.
But, he goes on, at one time:

斯道稍衰，姦僞以生，上下相犯。及其制禮，尊君卑臣，
君道剛嚴，臣道柔順，於是箴諫者稀，情志不通，故作
詩者，以道其美，而譏其過。[5]

The way [of earnest, friendly political criticism] died
away; wickedness and hypocrisy arose, and conflicts began
to exist between the upper and the lower. *Li* was then established to honor the prince and to subordinate the subject. The decorum of the prince was to be awesome and
that of the subject subservient; consequently there were
few [earnest and straightforward] advisers [criticizing
the prince], and the communication of feelings became
impossible. That was why some made poetry, in order to
spread [the prince's] virtue and criticize [his] vices [in
verse].

[2]See the *Yü shu*; the quotation is from K'ung Ying-ta, *Shang Shu cheng-yi*
(尚書正義), I,18a.

[3]夔曰，於，予擊石，拊石，百獸率舞 (K'uei said, "Alas, I smite the
stone and clap the stone; the various animals lead one another on to
dance").

[4]See the preface to his *Shih-p'u*, quoted in Hu P'u-an (胡樸安), *Shih Ching
hsüeh* (詩經學), p 7.

[5]*Liu-yi lun* (六藝論), quoted in Hu P'u-an, *Shih Ching hüeh*, p. 8.

As a result all the songs in *Shih Ching* are to Cheng Hsüan some-what esoteric and cryptic, with great messages underneath the surface to instruct, to criticize, or to eulogize. The elucidation of these messages becomes his primary task, and his approach is bound to be oblique. The literal meaning does not count for an allegorist commentator; the aesthetic implication is scarcely attended to. Nevertheless, Cheng's suggestion that the evolution of poetry is marked by the shift of the maker's association from music to ethics is unfounded. Cheng asserts that the former produces pri-mitive songs whereas the latter gives rise to sophisticated poetry: this is an entirely unwarranted statement. To restore the *Shih Ching* poem to the pre-Cheng tradition, that is, to reestablish its relation with music, will increase our ·chance of grasping the real aesthetics of the poem.

The "Great Preface" to *Shih Ching*, though noting the ethical function of poetry, associates poetry with music rather than pro-priety (which is Cheng Hsüan's *li*)[6]. The *Rites of Chou* initiates the categorization of "*liu shih*" (六詩), *feng, fu, pi, hsing, ya, sung,* which are said to be altogether and separately handed down by the "Grand Master."[7] And in another section of the book the *liu shih* are again mentioned in connection with singing, *liu shih chih ko* 六詩之歌.[8] The original bearing of *liu shih* is apparently related to the musical technicality. That *feng, ya, sung* differentiate melodic tempo, hence poetic rhythms, while *fu, pi, hsing* specify the three modes of rhetorical device is a demonstrable assumption.[9] Further,

[6]禮, which Cheng stresses in his treatise of early Chinese poetry (cf. note 4 above), denotes the principles of propriety rather than ritual or festivity. The latter has been thought by a great number of critics to be either the source of poetry or the occasion that helps to shape it. See Shih-hsiang Chen, "The *Shih-Ching:* Its Generic Significance in Chinese Literary History and Poetics," pp. 371–413. Representative discussions of English literature based on the similar belief are Jessie L. Weston, *From Ritual to Romance* (Cambridge, 1920); and John Speirs, *Medieval English Poetry: the Non-Chaucerian Tradition.* For criticism of this attitude towards medieval English literature, see C. S. Lewis, "The Anthropological Approach," pp. 219–230.

[7]*Chou Li* (周禮), *SSCCS,* XXIII, 13a.

[8]*Ibid.,* 18b.

[9]Wang Kuo-wei demonstrated that the poetic rhythm of the *Chou sung* section is relatively slower, hence more solemn, than that of other sections. See "*Shuo Chou sung*" (說周頌), in his *Wang Kuan-t'ang hsien-sheng ch'üan-chi,* Vol. I, p. 95. See also, Fu Szu-nien (傅斯年), "*Chou sung shuo*" (周頌說),

the *Record of Rites* mentions how a particular master of music expounds to Tzu-kung, a disciple of Confucius, the secret of singing the different song-tunes in accordance with appropriate moods and occasions.[10] For a period of time, we can assume, the singing of the *Shih Ching* poems was monopolized by specialists. Confucius remarks:

師摯之始，關雎之亂，洋洋乎盈耳哉！

From Master Chih's prelude to the *Kuan chü* finale, how magnificently it filled the ears!　　　　(*Analects* VIII, 15)

And the appointed singers whose names appear in the *Analects* number more than half a dozen. Although Confucius once suggests in vague words to the grand master of Lu how to perform music, he reveals himself in other places to be more a musicologist than a performer.[11] The Confucian scholars were also learning to sing the poems of *Shih Ching;* but rather than singing for ceremonial occasions or ritualistic purpose, they did it for the purpose of moral cultivation. The emphasis on thematic explication in the history of *Shih Ching* scholarship started with the Confucian school. Prior to this shift of attitude, musical decorum was the primary concern in all the treatments of either *shih* or *Shih Ching*.

Not only is poetry as music frequently discussed in connection with the rules of propriety in the *Analects* (e.g., III, 20; VIII, 8; XIII, 5; XVI, 13; XVII, 11, 18), but the passages cited from *Shih Ching* are often seriously commented on by Confucius using a purely ethical approach (e.g., III, 8; IX, 30). In Confucius' school the formal aesthetic interest of *Shih Ching* decreases and the ethical implications are commended to the student's attention. The scrutiny of the "six song-tunes" is no longer a subject in the school; but the thematic imports, their practical functions in the establishing of an ideal humanist scholar, are heeded:

詩可以興，可以觀，可以群，可以怨，邇之事父，遠之
事君；多識鳥獸草木之名。

Poetry [of *Shih Ching*] helps you to feel uplifted, to con-

---

in his *Fu Meng-chen hsien-sheng chi,* Vol. II; and Chen, "Generic Significance," pp. 381n., 383.

[10] *Li Chi* (禮記), *SSCCS*, XXXIX, 22.

[11] *Analects* III, 23.

template, to become sociable, to express grievance; at first you learn from it how to serve your father, and furthermore to serve your prince. Through it you get familiar with the names of birds, beasts, plants, and trees.

(*Analects* XVII, 9)

The classic was a subject taught for practical benefits, because "If one does not learn poetry, one will not be fit to converse with" (*Analects* XVI, 13). Confucius feels especially delighted to talk about poetry with his disciple Tzu-hsia because Tzu-hsia is able to link poetry with the principles of propriety and ceremony (*Analects* III, 8). This is the essence of the "poetry education" (詩教) as termed in the *Record of Rites*. Thus, to the Confucian school the charm of *Shih Ching* lies mainly in its thematic implications, which serve as illustrations for the ethics the school upholds. "Thoughts" are the focal point of their analysis; the Master says: "One sentence would embrace all the three hundred [*Shih Ching*] poems—having no depraved thoughts" (*Analects* II, 2). Chu Tzu-ch'ing (朱自清) summarizes the Confucian attitude towards poetry thus: "The age of Confucius witnessed the change of the function of *shih*: from the musical to the ethical."[12]

It was not until the Han age, however, that the thematic investigation became the all important concern of the major and lesser *Shih Ching* scholars. But the man who stands out in the crucial period of transition is Hsün-tzu (荀子). Hsün-tzu was credited by Wang Chung (汪中) as the Confucian thinker who comprehensively handed down the classics through the tumultuous age of the Warring States.[13] The *Shih Ching* corpus under our consideration is based on the early transmission executed by Mao Heng (毛亨), a disciple of Hsün-tzu. The first scholar of the great Mao tradition was Mao Ch'ang (毛萇), who, in competition with students of other transmissions, practically established the Mao texts as orthodox through his faithful, erudite elaboration on the annotations inherited from Mao Heng.[14] Commenting on this particular transmitted text, Cheng Hsüan, who had rejected other trans-

[12]*Shih-yen-chih pien* (詩言志辨), p. 125.
[13]*Shu hsüeh pu-yi* (述學補遺), *SPTK*, 5b–14a.
[14]For the assumption that the extant *Annotations* is an accumulated work contributed to by Mao Heng and Mao Ch'ang, see Wang, *ch'üan-chi*, Vol. IV, pp. 1227–1231.

missions and chosen to follow the Mao school in the strictly Confucian spirit, brought in for the thousand years to come his allegorical interpretations. Curiously, although Cheng improved and
enlarged the elucidation of the thematic imports of *Shih Ching*, he
did not show interest in clarifying any aspect of the formative
problem, such as the meaning of *hsing*. The cessation of the mini-
mum interest in the *hsing* problem may also be a sign of the decline
of music (*yüeh*), which is held by Confucius to be an integral part
of poetry. The probability that music had already died away and
the principles of propriety survived could explain why the decisive
growth of allegorism occurred after the Ch'in dynasty. The
attention directed to the study of form was subsequently all sup-
pressed. Henceforth, even when *fu*, *pi*, *hsing* were noted, the commentator's sensibility was dissociated from "music," and the virtual
aim was to let *fu*, *pi*, *hsing* confirm or illuminate all the different
allegories. With such an allegorical tradition so dominating *Shih
Ching* studies that aesthetics seldom has been considered, to read
the poems anew would be difficult if we confined ourselves to the
traditional "*fu-pi-hsing*" approach. An adjusted method is badly
needed. I would suggest that a close examination of the recurring
stock phrases scattered throughout the corpus may enhance our
understanding of the poems as they must have originally been
apprehended.

THE STOCK PHRASES

That the Chinese scholarly mind is in search of an ever-expanding
world of literary beauty is reflected in the change of its attitude,
generation after generation, toward the so-called stock phrases
of *Shih Ching*. There are interruptions and confusions, of course. But
the constantly modified methods devised for the appreciation of
the classical lyrics and sometimes for "words" themselves through the
recognition of stock phrases remain and are the basis of this study.

The last three stanzas of the six-stanza poem 168 are as follows:[15]

[15]The numbering of the poems follows William Hung et al., eds., *A Concordance to Shih Ching*. The poem, and other poems from *Shih Ching* cited in
the present study, are romanized in modern pronunciations to approximate
the sounds as apprehended by contemporary readers of the poetry. For
a reconstruction of the archaic reading more pertinent to some aspects of
analysis, see, for example, Bernhard Karlgren, *The Book of Odes*.

(4) 昔我往矣，黍稷方華； *hsi wo wang yi, shu chi fang hua*;
今我來思，雨雪載塗。 *chin wo lai szu, yü hsüeh tsai t'u.*
王事多難，不遑啟居； *wang shih tuo nan, pu huang ch'i chü*;
豈不懷歸？畏此簡書。 *ch'i pu huai kuei? wei tz'u chien shu.* 31–32

(5) 喓喓草蟲，趯趯阜螽。 *yao yao ts'ao ch'ung, t'i t'i fu chung.*
未見君子，憂心忡忡； *wei chien chün tzu, yu hsin ch'ung ch'ung*;
既見君子，我心則降。 *chi chien chün tzu, wo hsin tse chiang.*
赫赫南仲，薄伐西戎。 *ho ho nan chung, po fa hsi jung.* 39–40

(6) 春日遲遲，卉木萋萋， *ch'un jih ch'ih ch'ih, hui mu ch'i ch'i,*
倉庚喈喈，采蘩祁祁。 *ts'ang keng chieh chieh, ts'ai fan ch'i ch'i.*
執訊獲醜，薄言還歸； *chih hsün huo ch'ou, po yen huan kuei*;
赫赫南仲，玁狁于夷。 *ho ho nan chung, hsien yün yü yi.* 47–48

(4) Long ago when I was taking leave,
    The wine-millet and cooking-millet were in flower.
    Now as I am returning,
    Fallen snow covers the road.
    The king's business brings us so many hardships,
    I had no time to rest, or to bide.
    Did I not long to go home?
    I feared the inscriptions on the tablets. 30

(5) Dolefully chirp the cicadas;
    Jump and skip the grasshoppers.
    "When I could not see my lord,
    My heart was sad, never at rest.
    But now that I have seen my lord,
    My heart is still, finally at ease."
    Awesome, awesome is Nan-chung:
    He has also stricken the Western barbarians! 40

(6) The spring days are long, drawing out,
    Plants and trees exuberant in leaf;
    Orioles sing tunefully in harmony,
    And asters are being gathered, in abundance.
    We have captured and tried the culprits,
    And now I am on the way home.
    Awesome, awesome is Nan-chung:
    He has leveled down the Hsien-yün.

Almost every verse in the quotation appears once or several times elsewhere in the corpus. The Han annotators and commentators, nevertheless, leave this fact unnoticed. In considering the textual variants and parallels they devoted their scholastic attention mainly to the solution of the confusion among the independent transmissions, the Han (韓), Lu (魯), Ch'i (齊), and Mao versions, each followed by a substantial number of antiquarians.[16] Because of the early loss of the Han, Lu, and Ch'i texts, a fruitful comparison of the four rival transmissions is virtually impossible, unless one is content with a largely conjectural work. The *Cheng Commentaries*, oriented toward the elucidation of themes and intended to assure metaphorical relevancy in the succession of lines and stanzas, explain the cicada-grasshopper image in poem 168 as follows:

> 草蟲鳴，阜螽躍而從之，天性也。喻近西戎之諸侯聞
> 南仲既征玁狁，將伐西戎之命，則跳躍而鄉望之，如阜
> 螽之聞草蟲鳴焉。草蟲鳴，晚秋之時也，此以其時所見
> 而興之。[17]

> When cicadas sing, grasshoppers by nature jump towards them. This is to say that the feudal princes appointed near the Hsi-jung, hearing of Nan-chung's recent punishment of the Hsien-yün and his order to subject the Hsi-jung, were heartened, jumping around and looking forward to the forces to come: as do the grasshoppers when hearing the singing of the cicadas. Cicadas cry in late autumn. This [metaphor] is motivated (*hsing*) right at the time when one perceives [the scene].

Cheng does not seem to realize, or to care, that most of these verses also occur elsewhere with identical phraseology. On the one hand, he miserably confuses the meaning of *hsing*; on the other, the specification of the time as late autumn is a thematic deviation from the narrative development of the poem. The preceding stanza

---

[16]For a comprehensive study of the relation among the various transmissions, see Wang Hsien-ch'ien (王先謙), *Shih san-chia-yi chi-shu* (詩三家義集疏). Important contemporary studies include James Robert Hightower, "The *Han-shih Wai-chuan* and the *San Chia Shih*," pp. 241–310; also see Hightower, *Han Shih Wai Chuan*; and Lai Yen-yüan (賴炎元), *Han-shih wai-chuan k'ao-cheng* (韓詩外傳考徵).

[17]*Mao-shih Cheng chien* (毛詩鄭箋), *SPPY*, reprint (Taipei, 1967), IX, 10a. Yen Ts'an (嚴粲) considers this remark "extraneous;" see *Shih ch'i* (詩緝), XVII, 33a.

makes evident that the time when "I am returning" is late winter or early spring; furthermore, the stanza following the cicada-grasshopper paragraph points out that the expeditionary army marches back in the spring. Without referring to the existence of stock phrases, we would not be able to solve the problem of the time confusion, nor would Cheng. The inconsistency of time, being the result of composition by stock phrases resembling a mosaic, should indeed be taken as one of the characteristic signs of oral-formulaic poetry.[18]

In dealing with the last stanza of the poem, where the aster-gathering is ritualistically celebrated, K'ung Ying-ta (孔穎達) of the T'ang dynasty achieves another dimension of critical insight. In his *Rectification of the Orthodoxy*, he notes that the aster-gathering motif also comes in poem 154. "In the poem *Ch'i yüeh* [154]," K'ung remarks, "when the 'spring day' is mentioned, it specifies the third month: we are certain of this by referring to the context. One gathers asters to feed the silkworm; so everything here denotes that the time is in the third month."[19] Though he also supports the argument with internal evidence, K'ung by and large does not depart far from Cheng. That the aster-gathering motif is a formula and that the stanza in general is probably a composition by theme again go unnoticed. Actually, it is questionable whether the singer of poem 154 refers to the third month when he mentions the aster-gathering. Ch'en Huan (陳奐) maintains that this is performed in the second month.[20] Thus the context makes the time-specification doubtful, contradictory to K'ung's conception.

The Sung commentators do not make much improvement on earlier criticism of this aspect of the *Shih Ching* compositional art. Chu Hsi (朱熹) and Yen Ts'an (嚴粲), while occasionally observing that verses or terms also appear elsewhere, do not explain why repetition of phrases is a device of the ancient singer. To them, it seems, the recurring phrases prove nothing beyond plagiarism or

---

[18]Albert B. Lord and Francis P. Magoun, Jr. have demonstrated narrative inconsistencies as characteristic of oral epics. See Lord, "Homer and Huso II: Narrative Inconsistencies in Homer and Oral Poetry," p. 440ff; also his "Beowulf and Odysseus," pp. 86–91; and Magoun, "Two Verses in the Old English *Waldere* Characteristic of Oral Poetry," pp. 214–218.

[19]*Mao-shih cheng-yi* (毛詩正義), IX-4, 3b.

[20]*Shih Mao-shih-chuan shu* (詩毛氏傳疏), XVI, 16b (p. 424).

the cultivation of literary allusion.[21] And sometimes Chu would make conjectural remarks as does Cheng in the example quoted above.[22] The most oblique argument concerning the aster-gathering motif in the poem given above comes from Ou-yang Hsiu (歐陽修). In this poem, aster-gathering is mentioned immediately before the capture and trial of the culprits. Ou-yang exclaims, "Isn't it delightful" to try the barbarian chieftains in the floriferous spring-time, when plants are exuberant and rapidly flourishing, and birds are singing![23] By quoting it in his *Comprehensive Annotations,* Chu shows his agreement with Ou-yang. And at least one modern critic, Chu Tung-jun (朱東潤), approves this analogy.[24] On the other hand, since the Sung age, through the Ch'ing dynasty, philologists have adopted a new approach to the *Shih Ching* language. Normally they would group the stock phrases and through erudite comparison gloss particular terms or phrases with convincingly adequate references. Ch'en Huan, Yao Chi-heng (姚際恆), Ts'ui Shu (崔述), and Ma Jui-ch'en (馬瑞辰), for instance, through their new method, have contributed a great deal to archaic philology, although they only employ this method at random.[25] The great lexicographer Wang Yin-chih (王引之), in the name of his father Wang Nien-sun (王念孫), demonstrates the advantage of this method by grouping all the occurrences of the line *wang shih mi ku* (王事靡盬) in the whole corpus and concludes that *ku* is 息.[26] The finding is an important correction of the view which

---

[21]In the discipline of Old English literature, Claes Schaar, who criticizes the theory of oral-formulaic composition, is one of a group of scholars who maintain that passages which occur frequently "reflect literary borrowing." See Schaar, "On a New Theory of Old-English Poetic Diction," pp. 301–305. Also close to this opinion is Arthur G. Brodeur, *The Art of Beowulf,* esp. pp. 1–38.

[22]See esp. his comments on poem 121 in *Shih chi-chuan* (詩集傳), p. 277.

[23]*Shih pen-yi* (詩本義), VI, 8b.

[24]*Tu Shih szu-lun* (讀詩四論), p. 124.

[25]See, for instance, Yao Chi-heng, *Shih Ching t'ung-lun* (詩經通論), p. 174; Ts'ui Shu, *"Tu Feng ou-chih"* (讀風偶識), in his *Ts'ui Tung-pi yi-shu,* Vol. V, 5–6; Ch'en Huan, *Shih Mao-shih-chuan shu,* XVI, 3a (p. 397); and Ma Jui-ch'en, *Mao-shih chuan-chien t'ung-shih* (毛詩傳箋通釋), XVII, 5a.

[26]*Ching-yi shu-wen* (經義述聞), V, 22a. A contemporary Japanese Sinologist also notes in his edition of the *Feng* that the phrase is a "recurrent formula." See Yoshikawa Kōjirō (吉川幸次郎), *Shikyō Kokufū* (詩經國風), Vol. III, p. 358.

was held by Mao, Cheng, and the long train of their followers, including those eminents like K'ung Ying-ta and Chu Hsi. Early in this century, Wang Kuo-wei (王國維) showed that the scrutiny of stock phrases would also contribute to the dating of some significant poems. One piece of the evidence on which Wang dates the Shang hymns to the middle period of the Western Chou dynasty (circa tenth century B.C.) is that two verses of the hymns also, and only, occur in other Chou poems of that particular period.[27] Wen I-to (聞一多) carried on that scheme of study. His works have thrown much new light on *Shih Ching* scholarship. Many critics of today still find it comfortable to take Wen as a point of departure.[28]

However, up to this time, the existence of "stock phrases" has not been considered a particular phenomenon in terms of compositional art. In his commentary on poem 167, the nineteenth-century scholar Fang Yü-jun (方玉潤) insists that the willow and snow, which complete two formulaic systems, are what the soldier-singer sees at the different moments he goes to and comes back from the war. Otherwise, he contends, "the scene is not realistic; when the scene is not realistic, the poem is not good."[29] The so-called composition by formulas or themes never enters his mind. Probably Wen I-to was the first critic to notice that one of the many ways of reading the *Shih Ching* poem is through the observation of the formulaic system. In the outline for his unfinished edition of the *Feng* he discriminates the "poem" from the "song." He proposes:

1. The song: When incremental repetitions occur in several stanzas and variation appears only with rhyming words, take a horizontal approach, observing the varied words in stanzas and explain them collectively.

[27]Wang, *ch'üan-chi*, Vol. I, pp. 97–100. Eminent modern writings discordant with this dating include Fu Szu-nien, "*Lu sung Shang sung shu*" (魯頌商頌述) in his *chi*, Vol. II, p. 58ff; and Lu Hsün (魯迅), *Han wen-hsüeh-shih kang-yao* (漢文學史綱要) (Hong Kong, 1967), p. 15.

[28]Important *Shih Ching* studies of Wen are collected in his "complete works," *Wen I-to ch'üan-chi*, Vol. I, pp. 73–80, 117–138, 181–192, 339–367; Vol. II, pp. 67–208; also noteworthy is his unfinished edition of the *Feng* poems: see Vol. IV, pp. 5–94.

[29]*Shih Ching yüan-shih* (詩經原始), IX, 14a–15a (pp. 739–741).

    2. The poem: Take the vertical approach, word by word, and consider each stanza a unit.

    3. Combine the two.[30]

Once the musical component is noted, the chance of understanding these poems increases. Wen did not live long enough to elaborate on what he had suggested in his vague scheme. It would be fool-hardy to presume that he was on the verge of reading the poems as "oral-formulaic" compositions. Contemporaneous with and comparable to Wen's attempt to read the poems "horizontally" was the view of many other critics that the many ending words which are substituted one for another in accord with the rhyming systems are sometimes "meaningless." The foremost of these critics is Ku Chieh-kang (顧頡剛). Their treatment of what we might call the "formulaic system" in terms of rhyming, however, is merely a by-product of their polemics concerning the nature of *hsing*.[31] But none of these critics ever breaks away from the traditional *"fu-pi-hsing"* classification in their debates concerning the problem of the "variable words in the rhyming position."

The thirties of this century were a time of considerable progress in the study of the *Shih Ching* poetics. Chu Tung-jun groups a number of verses which contain the word *yu* (憂: grief; melancholy; mournful), in order to look into "the poet's mind," as he claims. The data are well prepared, but Chu does not utilize them. His conclusion is no more than that "sorrow gives birth to poetry."[32] In the field of historical criticism, Fu Szu-nien (傅斯年), in addition to issuing sundry papers, contributed his seminal treatise, the *Shih Ching chiang-yi kao,* which critics still hold in respect.[33] The ritualistic origin of a portion of the anthology comes to light through Wen I-to's anthropological approach, and many crucial issues in the traditional *Shih Ching* scholarship were modified in the modern

---

[30] Wen, *ch'üan-chi,* Vol. IV, pp. 6–7.

[31] See the second section of *Ku shih pien* (古史辨), Vol. III, esp. pp. 672–705. For Ku's contention that most of the *hsing* lines are "meaningless," see pp. 332–339, *passim.* For a survey of the issue and important additions to the understanding of *hsing,* cf. Chen, "Generic Significance." Cf. also, Lawrence A. Schneider, *Ku Chieh-kang and China's New History* (Berkeley, 1971), pp. 174–181.

[32] Chu, *Tu Shih szu-lun,* pp. 142–148.

[33] See his *chi,* Vol. II.

context by Chu Tzu-ch'ing.[34] Moreover, the participation of some
Western and Japanese scholars, writing in their own languages,
has made vivid a scene which would have been much dimmer
without them. As far as I can recognize, Arthur Waley is the most
sensitive, perceptive English reader among them. His translation,
The Book of Songs (an unrivaled combination of poetry and scholarship), presents in footnotes a number of "formulas." One of them is
what he calls the "bridal-hymn formula" which occurs in poem
168, among others:

未見君子，	Before I saw my lord
憂心忡忡；	My heart was full of grief.
既見君子，	But now that I have seen my lord
我心則降。	My heart is still
	(Waley's translation)[35]

Further, Waley has demonstrated how, by identifying particular
formulas and themes, our critical insight may be intensified and our
appreciation improved. In a footnote to poem 156, he displays an
admirable critical capacity: "This song is a typical 'elliptical
ballad,' in which *themes* are juxtaposed without explanation.
Thus 'the oriole . . .' down to 'all things proper have been done
for her,' is a *marriage-song theme*, which lets us know that during the
soldier's absence his wife has assumed his death and married
again."[36] Waley is probably the first of all the *Shih Ching* readers
to illuminate the aesthetic bearings of a poem through the observation of its formulaic language. More recently, Shih-hsiang Chen
(陳世驤) also contributed to the recognition of the *Shih Ching*
"stock phrases." In his study of *hsing*, the lines containing the
cicada-grasshopper motif and those termed by Waley the "bridal-
hymn formula," occurring in succession in poem 168, are taken as
evidence that "[*hsing* lines] had stemmed from a common source
of old generic convention, and not 'what the poet saw' at the moment of individual inspiration." For those lines, he remarks,
recur "elsewhere as stock phrases."[37] W.A.C.H. Dobson, on the

[34]In his *Shih-yen-chih pien.*
[35]*The Book of Songs*, p. 125.
[36]Italics mine. *Ibid.*, p. 117.
[37]Chen, "Generic Significance," p. 401.

other hand, takes the stock phrases to support his assumption that the *Shih Ching* poems were created in four successive stages, and that the existence of the "formulaic phrases" indicates the later poet's deliberate "citation and adoption" from works of the earlier.[38] At this point, Dobson meets the Old English scholar Claes Schaar, whose opinion that formulas and themes reflect "literary borrowing" has received criticism from David K. Crowne.[39] Later I will attempt to invalidate Dobson's assumption with external evidence and statistics on stylistic variation based on textual examination.

So far in the history of *Shih Ching* scholarship, with few exceptions, the stock phrases and type-scenes have not received sufficient notice. Scholars either ignore them or use them for various purposes, few of which pertain to the compositional art of poetry, poetry probably of a great "oral" tradition. Once the stock phrases enter the service of the lexicographer, for example, their poetic vitality diminishes. My intention is to treat them as the essential force in the making of the *Shih Ching* poem and to call them, instead of "stock phrases," *formulas*. I assume, first, that serious attention should be paid to the musical elements, and second, that only through the study of form can we wholly apprehend the bearings of a poem. The theory of oral-formulaic composition advanced by Milman Parry and Albert B. Lord in their studies of the European epic is my point of departure.

THE THEORY OF ORAL-FORMULAIC COMPOSITION

Referring to Homeric scholarship prior to Milman Parry, Albert B. Lord says, "It is a strange phenomenon in intellectual history as well as in scholarship that the great minds, . . . which could formulate the most ingenious speculation, failed to realize that there might be some other way of composing a poem than that known to their own experience."[40] The specific way of composing a poem that Lord implies here is what we call "oral-formulaic composition."

[38]"The Origin and Development of Prosody in Early Chinese Poetry," p. 231.

[39]For Schaar's theory, see note 21; for Crowne's criticism, see "The Hero on the Beach—an Example of Composition by Theme in Anglo-Saxon Poetry," pp. 362–372.

[40]*The Singer of Tales,* p. 11.

To affirm that the Homeric poems, first of all, were composed orally by formulas and themes has been a great intellectual experience for Parry, Lord, and their followers. According to Parry himself, he was indebted for his interest in the formulaic aspect of Homer to Antoine Meillet, upon some remarks of whose *Les Origines indo-européennes des mètres grecs* (Paris, 1923), Parry's first thesis on this issue, *L'Épithète traditionnelle dans Homère*, had its basis.[41] His further attempts to define the methodology were made with the publication of two monumental papers in the early thirties, one on the Homeric style as formulaic and the other more specifically on the Homeric language as the language of an oral poetry.[42] He also contended that "a true understanding of the Homeric poems could only come with a full understanding of the nature of oral poetry,"[43] a statement which he and Lord made later on the basis of their findings in field work in Yugoslavia in 1933 and 1934–1935. Even before the second trip to Yugoslavia, Parry had affirmed the basic axiom of his methodology for the modern inquiry into Homeric poetry, that the investigation of form is considered essential: "That literature falls into two great parts [is] not so much because there are two kinds of culture, but because there are two kinds of *form: the one part of literature is oral, the other written.*"[44] Parry believes that if we want to use one poetry for the understanding of another, we have no other way than "by starting from the form."[45] The fact that by analyzing twentieth-century survivals of Yugoslav songs Parry and Lord have advanced our understanding of the classical Greek epic proves that the study of form is primary in the discipline of comparative literature. "Using form as the clue to function, and style as establishing the character of thought," James A. Notopoulos

[41]Paris, 1928. This and all other papers of Milman Parry are collected in a book entitled *The Making of Homeric Verse: The Collected Papers of Milman Parry*, edited by Adam Parry.

[42]Milman Parry, "Studies in the Epic Technique of Oral Verse-making, I: Homer and Homeric Style," pp. 73–147; and "Studies in the Epic Technique of Oral Verse-making, II: The Homeric Language as the Language of Oral Poetry," pp. 1–50.

[43]Milman Parry and Albert B. Lord, *Serbo-Croatian Heroic Songs*, Vol. I, p. 3.

[44]"Whole Formulaic Verses in Greek and Southslavic Heroic Poetry," p. 180.

[45]*Ibid.*, p. 182.

thinks, is one of the most remarkable achievements of Parry as a Homerist.[46]

Concerning the early poems in general, Parry, and Lord too on a later occasion, ventured to dismiss old nomenclatures such as *primitive, popular, natural,* and *heroic.* The basic quality of early poetry, Parry suggests, is *oral.* The overall character of the language of oral poetry, he says, is "formulaic and traditional." Parry believes that "the poet who habitually makes his poems without the aid of writing can do so only by putting together old verses and old parts of verses in an old way."[47] Nonetheless, the continual use of the old parts of verses in a traditional way is not necessarily a second-best on which the poet falls back when inspiration fails him, as we might tend to imagine today. Our criterion of good poetry precludes the "traditional" and accentuates the "original." But since oral-formulaic poetry is spontaneously composed, by and large, the meaning of originality in that poetry is different from what we understand as originality today, in a lettered society where poetry is written line by line and corrected over and over again before it is published. This is not to say that any attempt of ours to evaluate oral-formulaic poetry is impossible, but that in the reading of early poetry composed orally and formulaically, we must be alert not to be deceived by our modern critical canons, which in fact are also "traditional." We may resent conventional formulas in later writings, but in the handling of conventional formulas an oral poet can reach his sort of originality. Stanley B. Greenfield defines the originality in formulaic composition as "the degree of tension achieved between the inherited body of meanings in which a particular formula participates and the specific meaning of that formula in the individual context."[48] Lord also notices that a poet-singer's art consists "not so much in learning through repetition the time-worn formulas as in the ability to compose and recompose the phrases for the idea of the moment on the pattern established by the basic formulas."[49] The utilization of conventional phrases is by itself an artistic performance, in other words. When we deal with

[46]James A. Notopoulos, "Mnemosyne in Oral Literature," p. 465.
[47]"Whole Formulaic Verses," p. 181.
[48]"The Formulaic Expression of the Theme of 'Exile' in Anglo-Saxon Poetry," p. 205.
[49]*Singer of Tales,* p. 5.

poetry of this form, it is necessary to break with the criteria developed later for evaluating poetry of the other form, the written. This break is necessary because one of the purposes of literary criticism is to reintegrate the poetic force of a given piece. The poetic force of oral poetry is generated by and therefore rooted in the repetition of certain phrases; that force was once vital, and can still be appreciated in a convention other than ours. Without the courage to reform our inherited criteria of criticism for "written literature," we would not be able to agree with what Alain Renoir says in reference to Old English poetry: "If Old English poetry cannot be appreciated from the point of view of our own time, teachers of English literature ought to abandon it with all dispatch and turn it over to the linguists and antiquarians."[50] No "point of view of our own time" in studies of Old English poetry, and Homeric as well, would perhaps be as dependable as Renoir thinks, had it not also been established on the basis of the oral-formulaic composition theory.

Through a presentation of the internal evidence, for example, the noun-epithet phrases in the *Iliad* and the *Odyssey*, Parry concludes that Homer was one of the early poets who composed orally by means of formulas. This affirmation contradicts many a mistaken concept of the recurrence of the fixed phrases in literature of a presumably particular form.[51] As Lord says in retrospect, by defining the formula, "the ambiguity of 'repetition' was eliminated. . . . Furthermore, the opprobrium attached to 'cliché' and 'stereotyped' has been removed."[52] *The Singer of Tales* confirms the classic definition of the formula, advocated in 1930 by Parry: *"a group of words which is regularly employed under the same metrical conditions to express a given essential idea."*[53] The Homeric noun-epithets are good examples to illustrate the statement. Odysseus is "of many devices," for example: the epithet is "regularly employed under the same metrical conditions to express a given essential idea." For the phrase, πολύμητις 'Οδυσσεύς, always occurs at the end of a

---

[50]"The Self-Deception of Temptation: Boethian Psychology in *Genesis B*," in *Old English Poetry*, ed. Robert P. Creed (Providence, 1967), p. 65.

[51]For a survey of the older theories concerning the Homeric language, see Parry, "Studies, II," pp. 1–4, and Lord, *Singer of Tales*, pp. 7–11.

[52]*Singer of Tales*, p. 30.

[53]"Studies, I," p. 80; *Singer of Tales*, p. 4, p. 30.

line: it fills out the verse after the caesura after the first syllable in the fourth foot. And it occurs fifty times in Homer. Likewise demanded by the meter to express given essential ideas are the epithets of Athene, θεὰ γλαυκῶπις (goddess grey-eyed), of Hector, μέγας κορυθαίολος (great flashing-crested), and so on.[54]

Another important finding is the "formulaic system": the term denotes a group of formulas forming a substitution pattern. In Parry's definition, a system is "a group of phrases which have the same metrical value and which are enough alike in thought and words to leave no doubt that the poet who used them knew them not only as single formulas, but also as formulas of a certain type."[55] In *L'Épithète traditionnelle* and the first part of the "Studies" Parry has illustrated the definition with ample examples from Homer. Lord has explained it further, with materials drawn from the Yugolsav epics, in *The Singer of Tales*. Chinese counterparts in *Shih Ching* are many, and one chosen at random will match the pattern. The system "*yen ts'ai ch'i* (plant name)" follows:

$$
言采其\;—\;\begin{cases} 蕨(14/2) \\ 薇(14/3) \\ 蝱(54/4) \\ 莫(108/1) \\ 桑(108/2) \\ 賣(108/3) \\ 杞(169/3)\;(205/1) \\ 遂(188/2) \\ 蕢(188/3) \\ 芹(222/2) \end{cases}
$$

Lord believes that " the fundamental element in constructing lines is the basic formula pattern":

> There is some justification for saying that the particular formula itself is important to the singer only up to the time when it has planted in his mind its basic mold. When this point is reached, the singer depends less and less on learning formulas and more and more on the process of substituting other words in the formula patterns.[56]

The theme is probably more important than anything else in the investigation of the aesthetic implications of oral-formulaic poetry. "By theme," Lord says, "I refer to the repeated incidents and

[54]*L'Épithète traditionnelle dans Homère,* pp. 13–18, *passim.*
[55]"Studies, I," p. 85.
[56]*Singer of Tales,* p. 36.

descriptive passages in the songs": his proposal, again, largely follows Parry's scheme.[57] A theme is an idea that comes into the singer's mind at the right time and almost irresistibly as he develops the "myth" of his song. The term *myth*, which is suggested by Robert Scholes and Robert Kellogg to denote "an articulated sequence of topoi"—*topoi* having the same meaning as *themes*[58]— is more desirable for our purpose than *story* or *plot* because it appears to embody better the internal development of both the narrative and the lyric poems. In addition, as Lord and other critics have acknowledged, the study of themes goes beyond the field of epic; the most interesting work, actually, has been done in the related fields of folk tale and myth, by Viktor Propp and Claude Lévi-Strauss, for example. In order to explicate the basic meaning of *theme*, I think we may have recourse to the topics derived from the modern studies of Old English poetry. The most vivid of Old English themes, are the "theme of Exile" described by Greenfield,[59] the "Hero on the Beach" suggested by David K. Crowne[60] and extended to cover the Middle High German epic by Renoir,[61] and the "Beasts of Battle" discovered by Francis P. Magoun, Jr.,[62] and reiterated and elaborated by Adrien Bonjour, Renoir, and Robert E. Diamond.[63] A brief observation of the theme affords us the opportunity to discern the oral art of composition by themes. Magoun states that the "Beasts of Battle" theme is "the mention of the wolf, eagle, and/or raven as beasts attendant on a scene of carnage."[64] He lists twelve occurrences of this theme in Old English poems:

[57]*Ibid.*, pp. 4, 68–98, *et passim.*

[58]*The Nature of Narrative,* p. 28.

[59]See "The Exile-Wanderer in Anglo-Saxon Poetry," and "Formulaic Expression of the Theme of 'Exile.' "

[60]"The Hero on the Beach."

[61]"Oral-Formulaic Theme Survival—A Possible Instance in the *Nibelungenlied*," pp. 70–75. Recent contributions to the study of this specific topic are Donald K. Fry, "The Hero on the Beach in *Finnsburh*," pp. 27–31, and "The Heroine on the Beach in *Judith*," pp. 168–184.

[62]"The Theme of the Beasts of Battle in Anglo-Saxon Poetry," p. 81.

[63]For Bonjour, see *"Beowulf* and the Beasts of Battle," pp. 563–573; for Renoir, see "*Judith* and the Limits of Poetry," pp. 145–155; For Diamond, see "Theme as Ornament in Anglo-Saxon Poetry," 461–468. Other important studies on the Anglo-Saxon epical themes include Lee Carter Ramsey, "The Theme of Battles in Old English Poetry," and Donald K. Fry, "Old English Oral-Formulaic Themes and Type-Scenes," pp. 48–54.

[64]"Theme of the Beasts of Battle," p. 83.

1. Battle of Brunanburg, 60–65a;   7. Finnsburg, 34–35a;
2. Beowulf, 3024b–3027;   8. Genesis A, 1983b–1985a;
3. Elene, 27b–30;   9. Judith, 204b–212a;
4. Elene, 110b–114a;   10. Judith, 294b–296a;
5. Exodus, 162–167;   11. Battle of Maldon, 106–107;
6. Finnsburg, 5a–7a;   12. The Wanderer, 81b–83a.

In each case specified above, no sooner is the battle referred or alluded to, than the singer mentions the beasts (*earn*, *hræfn*, and *wulf*), in order to "embellish a battle-scene," Magoun notes. All three beasts occur in 1, 2, 4, 9; in 5 and 6 (and somewhat similarly in 10) the wolf is mentioned specifically, and the birds are collectives as *here-fugolas*. Elsewhere only two of the triad are named: in 3 the wolf and the eagle; in 7 the raven and perhaps the eagle; in 11, ravens and an eagle; and in 12 a bird and the wolf. In 8 only one of the two birds is referred to, "though the theme is unmistakable."[65]

However, reference to the beasts does more than just "embellish a battle-scene"; it intensifies the various moods of the individual poems. In "Finnsburg," for instance, the mention of the raven is apparently unrealistic, for it follows the mention of the death of Guthlaf, one of the Danes, indoors. The Anglo-Saxon singer who composes by themes, nevertheless, makes use of the specific theme either because of its ready-made function of aggravating the carnage, "to elicit a conditioned response," as Renoir puts it,[66] or because he cannot resist it. In oral composition one image seems to generate another so spontaneously that inconsistency in narrative or lack of realism is often unavoidable. Also, Bonjour finds that in *Beowulf* 3020–3027 the beasts of battle are "briefly turned into a symbol of the ultimate triumph of death, the common destiny of dynasties, and the final fate of man. . . . So that the stirring contrast between the sound of the harp and the harsh voice of the carrion beasts really fuses the hackneyed theme into a haunting symbol of human transitoriness."[67] This is probably one of the most sophisticated speculations made by modern critics on the basis of the occurrence of a traditional theme in oral-formulaic poetry.

But we should also be on the alert for confusion between themes and prototypes. Generally speaking, themes are used by verse-

[65]*Ibid.*, p. 90.
[66]"*Judith*," p. 152.
[67]"*Beowulf* and the Beasts of Battle," pp. 569–570.

makers of the oral tradition, whereas prototypes are cultivated by
lettered poets. Even within the category of the recurrent beasts of
battle there is a difference between the beasts produced by the
theme and others developed in a prototypic system. Here we may
refer to the Chinese poetic tradition to make the point clear. Comparable references to the "Beasts of Battle" occur in *Shih Ching*: in
poem 178, for instance, the hawk (隼) is named prior to the out-
break of war. In the classic anthology per se, the occurrence of that
bird or any other beast with similar symbolic power is not sufficient
to make the composition of 178/3 thematic, but the bird motif in
connection with war henceforth becomes a prototype for other
poets to use. The address to the raven in the Han *yüeh-fu* heroic
poem, "Fighting South of the Wall" (戰城南) is an obvious use of
this prototype.[68] The Han poet, very likely a "folk singer," might
have the classical allusion in mind, but as soon as it is an allusion,
it is not a theme according to our definition. Nor was the T'ang
poet Tu Fu exercising any type of composition by themes when he
embellished his poem "For Kao Shih" (送高三十五書記) with
the familiar image:

飢鷹未飽肉	The hungry eagle has not eaten enough of the carrion
側翼隨人飛。[69]	Flapping the wings it follows men.

The poem contains a variation of the classical image, the prototype
of the warfare correlatives, rather than a theme as in an oral-
formulaic composition. The same is true of Li Po's exercise after the
very Han *yüeh-fu* poem, in which he incorporates the prototype of
the falcon pecking the bowels of a body (啄人腸).[70] Between the
Shih Ching poem 178 and the Han *yüeh-fu* military song there is an
interval of a thousand years, and there are another ten centuries
between the latter and Tu Fu and Li Po. That the beast in the
Chinese poems cited does not contribute to the making of a theme
in our sense is obvious; nor are the catalogue of fallen angels and
the council scene in *Paradise Lost* parts of the classical themes,

[68]Wang Hsien-ch'ien (王先謙), *Han nao-ko shih-wen chien-cheng*, (漢鐃歌
釋文箋正), reprint (Taipei, n.d.), pp. 25–28.

[69]*Tu-shih Ch'ien chu* (杜詩錢注) (Taipei, 1962), p. 2.

[70]*Fen-lei pu-chu Li T'ai-pai shih* (分類補注李太白詩) (Taipei, 1962), III,
14a.

though the council itself, in Lord's words, is "one of the most common and most useful themes in all epic poetry."[71] What the lettered poet utilizes are common prototypes and allusions which do not guide the myth but instead are submerged in it.

An oral poet normally has at his command a number of formulas and themes. Formulas are for constructing lines, usually following a metrical-grammatical system. Themes guide his thinking in the rapid process of composition to the making of the myth; that is, to the building of the larger structure. His is an art of manipulating themes and formulas to the maximum capacity so as to delineate spontaneously for the audience a myth—a myth of an event, or of an emotion, or both. On the one hand, themes elicit a "conditioned response" from the audience; on the other, they serve the singer as a mnemonic device. Formulas are comparable to allomorphs: they are fluid, forever changing in relation to situations and determined by them. The basic element of the language of oral-formulaic poetry, therefore, is "not the word but the phrasal pattern of a grammatical and metrical value, a 'grammetrical' unit," as R. F. Lawrence observes.[72] Guided by themes and regulated by grammetrical units or formulaic systems, an oral poet composes his poetry by means of traditional, fixed phrases. Except for the probability that the poet may have "a preverbal Gestalt," as Michael N. Nagler observes, which in the process of composing generates "a family of allomorphs,"[73] the poet's art also resembles that of a worker in mosaic, "placing in combinations pieces ready to his hands."[74]

APPLICATION OF THE THEORY

The theory of oral-formulaic composition is not verifiable until some sort of comparative approach is taken. At the early stage when Parry attempted to demonstrate what he called the "whole formulaic verse," he compared the Southslavic and the Homeric

[71]*Singer of Tales*, p. 68.

[72]"The Formulaic Theory and Its Application to English Alliterative Poetry," p. 170.

[73]See Michael N. Nagler, "Towards a Generative View of the Oral Formula," pp. 269–311.

[74]W. W. Lawrence, *Beowulf and Epic Tradition* (New York, 1963), p. 4.

poems. The theory was verified by being tested in more than one metrical tradition.[75] Lord carries on the method and enlarges it. *The Singer of Tales* contains investigations of diverse poetry produced in different environments and times, all treated within definite frame of analytic principles. With Parry and Lord, the only condition that governs the inclusion of a poetry to be inspected comparatively is the identification of form: the poetry must either be demonstrably "formulaic" or presumably "oral." Cultural matters such as genetic relations do not come into question.

As early as 1948 Lord showed a brief analysis of *Beowulf* 1473–1487 as oral-formulaic poetry to a medievalist who, departing with it, searched further and ever since 1953 has not only changed the general scene of Old English scholarship but also contributed to enriching the theory of oral-formulaic composition. The medievalist is Francis P. Magoun, Jr.; his initial study of this particular concern is his article "Oral-Formulaic Character of Anglo-Saxon Narrative Poetry," published in *Speculum*, XXVIII, 1953. The article is an expanded version of the second part of three lectures delivered by Magoun in London in 1952.[76] Although he was probably indebted to Lord's previous treatment of the *Beowulf* passage, Magoun deserves to be considered the first of the oral-formulaic scholars outside the classical context. For it was Magoun who seriously began to present Old English narrative poetry as oral-formulaic with sufficient reference to the Anglo-Saxon civilization. From Bede's story of Caedmon and Tacitus' description of the Germans, Magoun draws evidence to prove that the poetry in England for the seven centuries preceding Caedmon was oral. Oral, in turn, means "traditional and formulaic": at this point Magoun acknowledges his debt to Parry and Lord. In this article he discusses *Beowulf* 1–25 and *Christ and Satan* 512–535. He also confronts in passing the question of the problematic signed poems of Cynewulf. His conclusion is that the opening *Beowulf* passage is highly formulaic (nearly 70 percent), and the *Christ and Satan* passage likewise, though it is not comparable with the former. As for the reason that some phrases in both selections find no parallels, Magoun argues that it is be-

[75]*Singer of Tales*, p. 198.

[76]The article is reprinted in Donald K. Fry, ed., *The Beowulf Poet: A Collection of Critical Essays* (Englewood Cliffs, N.J., 1968), pp. 83–113. All references are to this reprint.

cause the extant Anglo-Saxon materials are limited. The case of Cynewulf's signed poems led Magoun to conceive of a "transitional period," a time when a poet like Cynewulf, both oral and lettered, would have composed by "dictating to himself, as it were, or to another person."[77]

To the prefatory article Magoun added in 1955 another which is fully devoted to the analysis of the Caedmonian *Hymn*. Bede thought the hymn miraculous, but Magoun finds it formulaic and traditional.[78] In the same year, he also published the seminal essay on the theme of the "Beasts of Battle," the essential meaning of which is discussed in the preceding section. The function of the specific theme, Magoun notes, is "ornamental." The discovery of the "Beasts of Battle" theme and the definition of the Anglo-Saxon "theme" have so attracted many disciplined minds in the field of oral-formulaic composition as to bother the original Parry-Lord concept. In *The Singer of Tales* Lord complains: "I should prefer to designate as motifs what they call themes and to reserve the term theme for a structural unit that has a semantic essence but can never be divorced from its form, even if its form be constantly variable and multiform." Even from this orthodox point of view, Lord thinks it is easy to discern some important themes in *Beowulf*, such as the repeated assemblies with speeches and the repetition of journeying from one place to another.[79] To Lord it does not seem sensible to differentiate "ornamental themes" from "essential themes," for when themes are not "essential," they are motifs. In the process of applying the theory to poetry of another cultural background new concepts are generated and the scope of the critical methodology widens. The particular critical attitude exemplified in Magoun's analytical terminology also has its drawbacks. The terminology tends to be confusing. The original meaning of "themes" is superceded by the revised one, the one which proves aesthetically exciting in the study of medieval European poetry as one cultural family. Renoir's supplying a Middle High German parallel of the "Hero on the Beach" theme, for example, is apparently motivated by vigorous interest in cultural rather than metrical

[77]*Ibid.*, p. 104.
[78]"Bede's Story of Caedmon: the Case History of an Anglo-Saxon Oral Singer," pp. 49–63.
[79]See pp. 198–199.

matters. Recently, Donald K. Fry offered to differentiate themes from type-scenes in order to solve the problem.[80] The original statement, which Lord reiterates in *The Singer of Tales*, nonetheless, remains unheeded in studies of medieval oral-formulaic composition. In her up-to-date reconsideration of oral tradition in Homer and Old English epic poetry, Ann Chalmers Watts calls the application of the theory for the study of the former to that of the latter "the imperfect application."[81] The use of the term *theme* is only one of numerous problems.

But basically, Old English scholars adopt and modify rather than dismiss the Parry-Lord theories. Lord in 1938 illuminated narrative inconsistencies as signs of "oral-formulaic" poetry;[82] Magoun completely agreed with him and helped to establish the axiom by offering "Two Verses in the Old English *Waldere* Characteristic of Oral Poetry" in 1958.[83] Similarly, in many other instances Old English scholars take advantage of the Homerist pioneer's findings, expanding and elaborating to build their Anglo-Saxon structure. Robert P. Creed's exhaustive investigation of *Beowulf* as oral-formulaic poetry, furthermore, earns Lord's praise as "complete, thorough, and accurate."[84] Meanwhile, Lord also acts as a supervisor, watching the various critical acts done in the name of the oral-formulaic methodology. Nagler reports that Lord has cautioned him, a Homerist, against the tendency of "falling back upon purely subjective evaluation of formulaicness" as represented by Wayne O'Neil's study of *The Seafarer*. Wayne O'Neil is the first Old English student suggested by Magoun to read the Old English elegiacs in the light of the Parry-Lord method.[85]

---

[80]See his "Old English Oral-Formulaic Themes and Type-Scenes," "Themes and Type-Scenes in *Elene* 1–113," pp. 35–45; the two articles on "The Hero on the Beach"; and "Aesthetic Application of Oral-Formulaic Theory: *Judith* 199–216a."

[81]*The Lyre and the Harp*. See esp. Chapter Three, pp. 63–125.

[82]"Homer and Huso II," p. 440ff.

[83]*Beiträge zur Geschichte der deutschen Sprache und Literatur*, LXXX: 214–218.

[84]Lord's critique (*Singer of Tales*, p. 198) is for Creed's "Studies in the Techniques of Composition of the Beowulf Poetry in British Museum MS. Cotton Vitellins A XV."

[85]See Nagler, "Towards a Generative View," p. 280. O'Neil's article on *The Seafarer* appears in *Speculum*, XXXV (1960), 596–600; his unpublished Ph.D. dissertation is called the "Oral-Formulaic Structure in Old English Elegiac Poetry."

The application is "imperfect" not only because of the metrical disparity that exists between the Homeric and the Old English works, but because their cultural backgrounds are different. The dubious role of Cynewulf bothers the Magoun school, and the meaning of *formula* in Old English poetry causes repeated polemics. In order to suit his purpose of investigating *Beowulf* as a whole, Creed, for example, modifies Parry's classic definition of the formula. Instead of "a group of words which is regularly employed under the same metrical conditions to express a given essential idea," Creed's definition of *formula* is as follows: "a word or group of words regularly employed under certain strictly determined metrical conditions to express a given essential idea." Consequently, *eald and unhar* is a formula (and in terms of alliterative verse it is a *reim-formel*); the verb-adverb group *gewat þa* is a formula; and a formula can be as brief as *þa*.[86] Only the first, *eald and unhar*, is acceptable to a strict Parryist. *Eald and unhar*, moreover, is an "epithet." "The presence of a highly organized, economical system of formulaic epithets in Homer very strongly supports the theory of oral composition," Watts notices, but such a system is largely absent from *Beowulf* and other poems. The Old English researchers have found phrases like *þæt wæs god cyning, billum ond byrnum,* and *grim ond grædig* comparable to the Homeric epithets, but their multiple purpose makes them equally unlike the latter. It is its distinctive metrical character that necessitates modifications in the attempt to affirm Old English poetry as formulaic composition. No matter how one tries to rewrite the definition of formula in the Old English context, it is hardly possible to link it any further with the original frame constructed by Parry and Lord. The critical act of application, in fact, is an act of modification.

In view of the runic signature in the Cynewulfian poems Magoun first speculates that there could have been a "transitional period" in the making of Old English oral poetry. Robert E. Diamond, another of his students, analyzes *Christ II, Elene, Juliana,* and the *Fates of the Apostles* in the context of the extant Old English documents, and finds that "they were composed in the traditional formulaic style." But Diamond refrains from assigning any certain

[86]See Creed, "The Making of an Anglo-Saxon Poem," pp. 445–454; reprinted with the author's "Additional Remarks" in Fry, ed., *Beowulf Poet,* pp. 141–153.

reason for the fact that a literate man should write in "entirely formulaic" style.[87] Many scholars oppose Magoun's assumption that Cynewulf "dictated his poems to himself." Among them Arthur G. Brodeur and Claes Schaar are most notable. Brodeur is the "chief proponent of the written theory," as his student Greenfield calls him; he has never acceded to the theory that formulaic poetry is orally composed. In the confusion that seems never to clear up, Larry D. Benson suggests that the study of formulas and themes need not be based on the Parry-Lord assumption. He sides with the written theorists: "Indeed, I believe that a recognition that Old English poetry is both formulaic and lettered would lead to an even more exciting and fruitful development in our discipline." Benson argues that the new attitude would mean "an aesthetic sympathy" of ours in reading the formulaic poems: "That Old English oral singers used a heavily formulaic style is only an attractive theory—probably true but necessarily unproven, that lettered poets, such as the author of the Boethian *Meters,* did use such a style is a demonstrable fact."[88] Benson's purpose in his important 1966 article is to dismiss the so-called touchstone of oral-formulaic composition in general and to question the existence of a transitional period as described by Magoun. By presenting the *Meters of Boethius* as highly formulaic, together with Diamond's analysis of the Cynewulfian group, he is on the verge of refuting the axiom that oral poetry is formulaic and vice versa. Despite Joseph Duggan's criticism in terms of "technical vocabulary," the case described by Benson has helped to direct our attention to the problem of "transitional period."[89] In our present study, an unprecedented application of the theory to classical Chinese poetry, an awareness of both problems would keep us from falling into the pit that has caught many Old English students.

There are many reasons to believe that the poems of *Shih Ching* have gone through a period of transmission, from an oral and perhaps very formulaic stage to what we see today, a version colored with scribal alterations and emendations. The scribal alterations at the first stage were probably not so slight as we are as willing to

[87]"The Diction of the Signed Poems of Cynewulf," esp. pp. 237–241.
[88]"The Literary Character of Anglo-Saxon Formulaic Poetry," p. 340.
[89]For Duggan's criticism of Benson, see *The Song of Roland: Formulaie Style and Poetic Craft,* pp. 30–33.

admit. Many early documents, presupposing that a great body of the songs were of folk origin "sung" among the people, state that there were officials whose duty was to collect songs and present them to the king:

> 孟春之月， 群居者將散， 行人振木鐸徇于路以采詩，
> 獻之太師，比其音律，以聞天子。故曰，王者不窺牖戶
> 而知天下。[90]

> In the early month of spring as those who lived together
> [for the winter] were about to disperse, the official mes-
> senger would shake a bell with a wooden tongue on the
> road to collect songs and then submit the songs to the
> grand master, who regulated them in accord with notes
> and tunes to present to the king. That is why we say that
> though a prince does not watch beyond the window and
> the door, he knows the world.

Between the song sung among the people and that accompanied with notes and tunes offered to the king, there is definitely a process of transmission. Many songs were edited and probably even rewritten to befit the specific musical and ceremonial atmosphere of the court. The documents of ritual practices in the early dynasties indicate that many an assembly was not considered complete without songs. Possibly, over a period of time tunes of various moods and import were fixed but the verses were not. A great number of verses must have once been composed to a specific tune, as subsequently also in the case of *tz'u* (詞) or *ch'ü* (曲).[91] Szu-ma Ch'ien reports that the compiler of *Shih Ching*, whether or not it was Confucius, had to venture to leave out duplicates and include only one-tenth of all the songs known to the compiler.[92]

Although superfluous verses concerning a common subject were usually rejected from the anthology, the compiler did not exclude

---

[90]Pan Ku, *Han shu* (漢書) (Peking, 1964), p. 1123. For discussions relating to this problem, see Ch'ü Wan-li (屈萬里), *"Lun Kuo-feng fei min-chien ko-yao te pen-lai mien-mu"* (論國風非民間歌謠的本來面目), pp. 477–491; and Ch'en P'an (陳槃), *"Pa..."* (跋 ...), and *"Ku-shih chih ts'ai-chi"* (古詩之采集), *BIHP*, XXXIV (1963), 493–504.

[91]For a comprehensive treatment of the problem concerning the *tz'u* and *ch'ü*, see Lu K'uang-ju (陸侃如) and Feng Yüan-chün (馮沅君), *Chung-kuo shih shih* (中國詩史), reprint (Hong Kong, 1961), Vol. III.

[92]*Shih chi* (史記), (Peking, 1964), p. 1937.

them entirely. To the same tune there are sometimes verses of
similar, if not identical, content. The three poems of warfare
against the Hsien-yün tribes (167, 168, 177), for example, have an
identical metrical pattern: each poem contains six eight-line verse
paragraphs, and each line four words (or "syllables"). Of the
selfsame metrical pattern, moreover, is poem 198, which is evidently a "complaint" and presumably composed during the reign
of King Yu (幽王), when two other important complaints attributed to the same period, poems 193 and 197, were made. Poems
193 and 197 are both patterned with the metrics described above,
except that each contains two more stanzas. All the poems (167,
168, 177, 193, 197, 198) are molded according to the structure of
poem 161, which has a much favored tune and is frequently referred
to in the books of rites. The titles specified for feasting occasions,
including those of poems 161, 162, 163, 170, 171, and 172, are
highly formulaic.⁹³ The poems now represented under these titles
in the *Shih Ching*, therefore, were apparently composed orally
by themes and formulas to the individual tunes. In other words,
the title of a tune finally became the title of one of the poems
composed according to it. And this must have taken place in
a period that we would call "transitional." Also, in the present
anthology there are some titles that have survived without verses.
These are, again, titles of tunes but not of any specific composi-
tions.⁹⁴ We may be quite certain that oral-formulaic composition
in the Parry-Lord sense was once practiced in ancient China. A
further discussion of this aspect will follow in the subsequent chapters, where formulas and themes are analyzed.⁹⁵

A group of the *H. Ya* poems in *Shih Ching*, furthermore, presents
a problem almost identical with that which complicates the Cynewulfian group. Poems 191, 200, 259, and 260 bear names of some
individual poets. The poets' names are palpably incorporated: in
191 a certain Chia-fu (家父), in 200 a senior appointee of an ob-
scure office in charge of the palatial affairs (寺人孟子), and in both
259 and 260 a Chi-fu (吉甫) whose name appears several times in

⁹³For a discussion of the formulaic nature of poem 162, for example, see
pp.122–125; also see Appendix B.
⁹⁴*Nan kai* (南陔), *Pai hua* (白華), *Hua shu* (華黍), *Yu keng* (由庚), *Ch'ung
ch'iu* (崇丘), *Yu yi* (由儀).
⁹⁵See Chapters Three and Four.

the songs of the Chou kingdom. These poems are similar in that
they are equally formulaic and in that they are traditionally dated
in the final years of the Western Chou dynasty. This declining period
of the Western Chou dynasty probably parallels the "transitional
period" of classical Chinese poetry when poems were written as
well as orally composed. Referring to their art, the poets themselves do not clearly specify whether they write or sing; instead,
they "make" (作), an ambiguous expression. Their works are
interchangeably referred to as *sung* (誦) and *shih* (詩). Although by
original implication both words pertain to musical expression, by
this time they specifically denote poetic works accomplished at
leisure.[96] In *Shih Ching*, unlike what we find in other sources, *shih* and
ko seem to have acquired their individual meanings already. Poem
252 shows that *shih* tends to specify the verbalization of the subject
matter, whereas *ko* signifies the act of singing it.

矢詩不多， [I] offer a great many *shih*,
維以遂歌。 All made for singing (*ko*).

So it is in many other places: whenever *ko* occurs, it refers to the act
of singing. Salient examples are found in poems 22, 56, 109, and
141. Also, the poems in which the expression *tso ko* occurs are normally more formulaic than those in which the expression *tso shih*
does. The most conspicuous example is the celebrated poem 162,
which we have pointed out as one of the poems undoubtedly best
described as bearing clear formulaic marks of earlier "oral improvisations." In conclusion, I would suggest that, in view of the fact
that *shih* instead of *ko* is mentioned in the four poems containing the
author's names (191, 200, 259, 260), these poems are lettered compositions, though they also have formulaic influences. There is no
other poem in the whole corpus of *Shih Ching* so complex in metrical
structure and peculiar in title as poem 200. It is known as *Hsiang
po* (巷伯), a specific title with intricate verbalization indeed for
better disclosing the special persona and his situation.[97] This is not
usual in the entitling of the *Shih Ching* poems, which, perhaps owing
to some compiler's ingenuity, usually take their titles directly from

[96]Cf. Shih-hsiang Chen, "In Search of the Beginnings of Chinese Literary
Criticism," pp. 45–64.
[97]Ma Jui-ch'en scrutinizes this problem with the most meticulous care.
See *t'ung-shih*, XX, 44b–45b.

some words appearing in the beginning lines. By and large, the title of a *Shih Ching* poem is given more for editorial convenience than for explicating the individual theme. In this concern, poem 200 is singular. The poem is also peculiar in stanzaic structure. It is comprised of four four-line, one six-line, one eight-line, and one five-line paragraphs—the least typical in the corpus. The stanzaic structure of the poem is especially irregular parhaps because it was not composed spontaneously by formulas to any fixed tune.

The foregoing arguments have been made in the hope of pointing out that there are good reasons for us to assume a "transitional period" in the making of *Shih Ching*. Many other poems are possibly related to this category, but I would attempt no conjectures. The problem of a transitional period is sometimes connected with the process of transmission. The story of Caedmon is an example.[98] Bede endeavored to take down in Latin the hymn reported to have been composed orally (*æt his muðe writon*), a poem which had doubtless lost its spontaneous character by the time Bede heard it. That is to say, we have no means of determining whether the hymn as Caedmon sang it in the presence of the angel was "formulaic" or not. By the time Bede heard it, it was; and that was apparently because the hymn had been handed down orally in a West-Saxon form. The period when it survived in the oral form also corresponded with a transitional period, as the hymn was being "transmitted" both psychologically by the oral singers and literarily by Bede. In its oral, alliterative form it reached the Alfredian translator, presumably Bishop Waerferth, and it did not seem to him to depart far from the Latin of Bede. The translator, certainly well disciplined in classic learning and familiar with the native vernacular tradition, like the author of the *Meters of Boethius,* concluded it in the form we see today.[99] As a result of three processes of transmission: one by Caedmon in retrospect, the other by Bede the scribe, and the third by Bishop Waerferth the translator—the hymn subject to Magoun's analysis is formulaic. Normally oral theorists suppose that the process of transmission, which involves writing, decreases the degree of a poem's formulaicness. The case of Caedmon, however,

[98]See Magoun, "Bede's Story of Caedmon."
[99]For a suggestion about the way the Alfredian translator carried through the *Hymn* of Caedmon in the Old English *History* of Bede, see C. L. Wrenn, *A Study of Old English Literature,* pp. 94–95.

shows that sometimes it is difficult to say whether the process of transmission decreases or increases it. For there was obviously a period when the lettered man actually welcomed traditional language and conventionalism in order to effect poetic communication.

That the *Shih Ching* poems under our consideration are particularly noted as a great, distinctive genre of lyrics raises another question. Is the oral theory, originally designed for the reading of epics, applicable to the Chinese "lyrics"? If so, this application, to a poetry of culturally unrelated and generically disparate nature, will become the newest frontier of the concept. Indeed, beyond the Parry-Lord scope there are a number of poetry which have been subject to study related to the theory. The method has been examined repeatedly in reference to many areas besides Old English narrative poetry, such as the Middle English metrical romance, the Gaelic, the Old French, and even some South Indian verses.[100] Magoun's analysis of Caedmon's hymn, though the first of all serious attempts to describe a lyric in terms of oral-formulaic composition, yields questions rather than conclusions. Before he actually inspected the problems in the hymn, Magoun had doubted if the oral theory would fit the study of short lyric poems.[101] Wayne O'Neil's thesis marks one of the most daring attempts in our field— reading the Old English reflective poems from the point of view largely defined by Magoun. O'Neil proceeds by first admitting that his materials are "generally non-narrative." But he thinks it worthwhile to try; he believes that such an attempt may prove that there

[100]Important works on poetry outside of the Parry-Lord field of investigation are listed in Scholes and Kellogg, *Nature of Narrative.* Nagler gives a number of others; see "Towards a Generative View," p. 272n. Other recent contributions in book form include Robert C. Culley, *Oral Formulaic Language in the Biblical Psalms,* William Whallon, *Formula, Character and Context: Studies in Homeric, Old English and Old Testament Poetry*; Ann Chalmers Watts, *The Lyre and the Harp*; and Adam Parry, "Introduction," in *The Making of Homeric Verse.* An article concerning literature farthest from the field of Parry but involving some criticism of the theory is Earl Miner, "Formula: Japanese and Western Evidence Compared," read in the 5th International Congress of the ICLA in Belgrade, 1967. Peter H. Lee utilizes the Parry concept of "formula" in his work in progress, *The Song of Flying Dragons,* which inspects the epical elements in a Korean dynastic history *written* (Lee emphasizes) in the fifteenth century. For a translation of Lee's subject, see *Songs of the Dragons* trans. James Hoyt. n. p. 1971.

[101]See "Oral-Formulaic Character of Anglo-Saxon Narrative Poetry," p. 103; and "Bede's Story," p. 53.

was a time when the lettered and unlettered traditions were "at very subtle play."[102] O'Neil sees the fact that the metrical features of the Old English narrative and reflective poems are the same as justifying the application of the method designed for the former to the latter. Besides, he says:

> Within the scheme of the narrative poetry we can find lyrical and elegiac passages which resemble the texture of the elegies enough to make us wonder if one might not have been an outgrowth from the other. In any event there is sufficient overlap in subject matter so that the elegies and narrative poems are in accord thematically.[103]

The arguments, apparently predicated upon cultural homogeneity, may justify O'Neil's position, but I am not using them to justify mine. For "sufficient overlap in subject matter" does not occur between the Old English narrative and the Chinese lyric poem.

But even before O'Neil's thesis was completed in 1960 there had been pioneering works carried out and published in the related scheme by James Ross and M. B. Emeneau.[104] Their subjects, respectively Gaelic and South Indian lyrics, are not confined to the cultural limits of the Parry-Lord-Magoun chain. These treatments nonetheless prove what Parry advocated in the thirties: "literature falls into two great parts not so much because there are two kinds of culture, but because there are two kinds of form." [105] As we have already stated, this is the major premise of the present study. It is unfortunate that Sir Maurice Bowra should have insisted that short poems do not call for formulas.[106] His speculation is hardly correct. For formulaic structure of poetry is not in any way related to length—the findings of Ross, Emeneau, O'Neil, and others concerning oral lyrics are sufficient to negate Bowra's assumption. Even the small historical verse "Edgar" in the *Anglo-Saxon Chronicle* of the year 959 admits phrases like *wide ond side* and *oft ond gelome* which are "epic formulas" found repeatedly in Layamon.[107]

---

[102]"Oral-Formulaic Structure in Old English Elegiac Poetry," p. 110.

[103]*Ibid.*, p. 111.

[104]James Ross, "Formulaic Composition in Gaelic Oral Literature," pp. 1–12; M. B. Emeneau, "Toda Dream Songs," pp. 39–44; and Emeneau, "Style and Meaning in an Oral Literature," *Language*, XLII (1966), pp. 323–345.

[105]See note 44.

[106]*Heroic Poetry*, p. 232, *et passim*.

[107]Cf. John S. P. Tatlock, "Layamon's Poetic Style and Its Relations," p. 10.

In his early writings defining the method of oral theory as a new concept for reading Homer, Parry agrees that oral-formulaic composition was probably also practiced in the lyric tradition of ancient Greece.[108] His supposition is proved true by J. A. Notopoulous and W. E. McLeod.[109] The Greek, the Old English, and other testimonies encouraged Robert C. Culley to analyze the psalms in the light of the oral theory.[110] Culley's work appears to be the most eloquent precedent for subjecting our present material, *Shih Ching,* to the comparative study of formulaic poetry. The biblical psalms, of all poetry hitherto tested against the theory, are the most nearly similar to our subject, in terms of historical and aesthetic importance. The biblical psalms are evidently not comparable to the *Shih Ching* poems in scope, but in range of subject matters and perhaps in generic significance they have shared the fate of being regarded as scriptures in the past. Culley's study has not only removed the mystic atmosphere surrounding the psalms, but also brought a broader perspective to the Parry-Lord theory. In the present study, while assuming the analysis of form as essential, I also attempt to verify a literary theorem and to illuminate the aesthetic implications of some important *Shih Ching* formulas and themes.

[108]"Studies, I," p. 92; "Studies, II," p. 29.

[109]Notopoulos, "The Homeric Hymns as Oral Poetry: A Study of Post Homeric Oral Tradition," *AJP*, LXXXIII (1962), 337–368; Notopoulos, "Studies in Early Greek Poetry," *HSCP*, LXVIII (1964), 1–77; McLeod, "Oral Bards at Delphi," *TPAPA*, XCII (1961), 317–325.

[110]*Oral Formulaic Language in the Biblical Psalms.*

TWO

The Formula: I

TOWARD A DEFINITION

The definition of the formula varies with respect to the individual linguistic features that determine an "acoustic pattern," for the pattern limits the meaning of a line or half-line of a given metrical tradition. Recent analysts of formulaic literature have questioned whether we can describe the nature of the formula without considering the "mental template in the mind" of the poet-singer.[1] Our understanding of the formula in the *Shih Ching* context, therefore, cannot be complete until the essence of classical Chinese prosody and the mode of that poetic intuition are examined.

There are 311 titles in the corpus of *Shih Ching*, of which 305 poems are extant. The number of verse paragraphs (or stanzas) in each poem is not consistent. It ranges from 1 to 16, the former being typical of all the Chou liturgic poems (31 altogether) and of 3 of the 5 Shang hymns. The 16-stanza structure occurs only once, in poem 257 in the *T.Ya* section. The anthology is traditionally divided into four sections. The average number of stanzas per poem in each section is represented in table 1.

TABLE 1:

AVERAGE NUMBER OF STANZAS PER POEM (BY SECTION)

Section	Number of Poems	Number of Stanzas	Number of Stanzas Per Poem
Feng	160	482	3.01
H. Ya	80	369	4.61
T. Ya	31	219	7.06
Sung ⎧ Chou	40 ⎧ 31	71 ⎧ 31	1.77 ⎧ 1
⎨ Lu	⎨ 4	⎨ 24	⎨ 6
⎩ Shang	⎩ 5	⎩ 16	⎩ 3.2

[1]Michael N. Nagler, "Towards a Generative View of the Oral Formula," p. 269.

35

The chart shows first that the liturgic hymns (*sung*) of the Chou house are uniform, each having one stanza, and except for three Shang hymns (301, 302, 303) no other poem in the corpus is similarly formed. The rest of the dynasty hymns (304, 305) of the Shang house and all the Lu verses (297–300) resemble more the poems of the *T. Ya* than the *Chou sung*, the latter being considered the earliest of all the extant works collected in *Shih Ching*.[2] The poetry of the Shang and the Lu houses resembles that of the *T. Ya* section not only in stanzaic, rhythmic, and metaphoric features, but also in the common tenor of their subject matter. Secondly, in reference to the traditional categorization, the average number of stanzas in each poem ranges from 1 to 7.06. Although in terms of historic development the Chou hymns (to which the lowest figure is related) are the "simplest" and earliest, we are not justified by the same token in labeling the *Feng* as most "sophisticated" songs. In terms of stanzaic structure, for instance, the *Feng* songs are midway between the liturgic verses of the Chou court and the dynasty hymns specified as *T. Ya*. Thus a close obervation of stylistic relationships in *Shih Ching* is sufficient to deny Dobson's theory that the evolution of early Chinese poetry is marked by a series of "successive stages," the *sung*, the *ya*, and then the *feng*, a series which, he thinks, also reveals a consequence of "transition from prose to poetry."[3]

The total of *Shih Ching* verses (lines) is 7284, distributed in 1141 stanzas.[4] The number of verses in each stanza also varies: from 2 (103/1,2,3; 170/4,5,6) up to 38 (300/4); the most common is 4. Table 2 shows the statistics of the overall *Shih Ching* structure at the stanzaic level.

Four-verse stanzas account for more than one-third (33.5 percent)

[2]See, for one, Fu Szu-nien, *chi*, Vol. II-B, pp. 18–44.

[3]See W.A.C.H. Dobson, "The Origin and Development of Prosody in Early Chinese Poetry," p. 231. The speculation that there is a phenomenon of "transition from prose to poetry" in ancient Chinese literature is unwarranted. Concerning the freer prosodic quality of the *Chou sung* verses, for example, Wang Kuo-wei has made an apology in terms of ancient ceremonial practice; see *Wang Kuan-t'ang hsien-sheng ch'üan-chi*, Vol. I, pp. 93–95. Though Wang's view is countered by Fu Szu-nien (see note 2), both believe that "prose" would not be the word for the unrhymed liturgics of the Chou court.

[4]The figure is based upon the paragraphing defined by K'ung Ying-ta, who actually departs from the orthodox *Cheng Commentaries* (which the *Harvard-Yenching Concordance* follows), in *Mao-shih cheng-yi*.

TABLE 2:
NUMBER OF STANZAS OF DIFFERENT LENGTHS

Stanza(s) of			
2 verses	6	12	46
3	28	13	2
4	382	14	7
5	62	15	2
6	240	16	1
7	56	17	1
8	215	22	3
9	19	23	1
10	59	31	1
11	9	38	1
		total:	1141

of the total. Allowing that the six-verse stanza is primarily a sort of expanded four-verse stanza and that the eight-verse stanza is a fusing of two four-verse stanzas, the number of stanzas of basically four-verse pattern rises to more than two-thirds (73.2 percent) of the grand total.[5] It is not dangerous, therefore, to take the four-verse stanza as the fundamental pattern of paragraphing of the *Shih Ching* prosody.

A verse paragraph is the metrical, rhetorical fulfillment of poetic unity. This is true in early Chinese poetry and in lyric poetry generally. Presumably it is in view of this principle that K'ung Ying-ta ventures to alter the established doctrine of paragraphing set forth by Cheng Hsüan. In his "rectification" on the first poem (*Kuan chü*), for example, K'ung notes that the poem is comprised of 3 stanzas instead of 5, and he claims that the modification is done in the interest of restoring the poem to the original design of Mao. Chu Hsi abandons the remnants of the *Cheng Commentaries* altogether, deciding that the poem is a composition of three paragraphs, including 1 four-verse and 2 eight-verse stanzas.

We have come to the point where *verse* must be defined. A verse is a succession of words arranged according to metrical and semantic rules as a unit. In *Shih Ching* it varies in length and is determined rather in its syntactic than in its rhyming value. Normally, a *Shih*

[5]See K'ung's discussion on the paragraphing of poem 1, *ibid.*, I–1, 14b.

Ching verse does not run on simply to suit a particular rhythmic
pattern; in other words, enjambement is completely absent. As
a consequence a verse is protean, varying in the number of syllables
though the basic structure is not hard to recognize. Traditional
scholars have tended to determine the length of a verse on the basis
of semantic completeness, supplemented with observation of the
rhyming pattern which does not always exist. That is to say, whereas
we can almost always rely upon scansion to discern a verse in
Homeric, or a half-verse (hemistich) in Anglo-Saxon, poetry, in
Shih Ching, we often have to rely upon semantic analysis to determine whether a succession of words is a verse. Metrical scansion, if
meaningful at all, is not fundamental in the reading of a *Shih Ching*
poem, because the scheme of meter in the classical anthology is
not evident when approached through counting of syllables.

As the Chinese language is largely monosyllabic, when we call a
verse *four-word*, we refer to a verse of four syllables. The majority
of the *Shih Ching* verses are four-word verses, but all types of variety
are present. Some researchers have argued that in a few instances
even a single word forms a verse. The following list shows the *Shih
Ching* verse in its various lengths:

1. 儆，還 (75)； 予 (185)； 歆 (245).[6]
2. 祈父 (185)； 肇禋 (268)； 鱣鯊，鰋鯉，魴鯉 (170).
3. 綏萬邦，婁豐年 (294)；江有沱 (22)；醉言舞 (298)；叔于田 (77).
4. 關關雎鳩 (1).
5. 誰謂雀無角 (17)； 外大國是疆 (304)； 君子有孝子 (247).
6. 嘉賓式燕以敖 (161)； 我姑酌彼金罍 (3)； 室人交徧摧我 (40)；
   狂人之狂也且 (87).
7. 以燕樂嘉賓之心 (161)； 如彼築室於道謀 (195)； 尚之以瓊華乎
   而 (98).

[6]K'ung Ying-ta, *ibid.*, like many other important commentators, notes
that a single word does not make a verse. "A verse should mean a succession
of words." He adds, "No word-group comprised of less than two words"
is a verse. However, approaching mainly from the metrical point of view,
many scholars contend that K'ung's notion is not necessarily authoritative.
See Ku Yen-wu (顧炎武), *Jih-chih lu* (日知錄), XXI, p. 66; and his *Shih
pen yin* (詩本音), III, 1b, for the defence of the citations from poem 75.
See Hao Ching (郝敬), *Mao-shih yüan-chieh* (毛詩原解), 1891, preface-
32b, for the reason why the cited word from 245 should be considered a
verse by itself.

8. 我不敢傚我友自逸 (193)；　胡瞻爾庭有懸貆兮 (112)；　十月蟋蟀
   入我牀下 (154).

9. 泂酌彼行潦挹彼注兹 (251)；　二后受之成王不敢康 (271).[7]

In determining the number of words (or syllables) that makes up a
verse, we must perhaps take particles into consideration; for particles
(e.g., 且 in item 6 and 兮 in item 8) are counted in the pitch of
a song, and the principle of music is our concern too. In other
words, particles are syntactically important in the making of
the *Shih Ching* poem, although perhaps not equally essential in
semantics. Thus understood, we take the verse *ch'ing yang wan hsi*
清揚婉兮 to be comprised of four words. And it is imaginable that
the particle therein is well recognized in the course of singing,
although it is omitted in all the books of *Shih Ching* scansion, for
example, in the work of Ting Chu-yün (丁竹筠).[8]

In view of the fact that interjections such as *hsi* 兮, *yi* 矣, *tsai* 哉
are used in most cases to fulfill metrical rather than semantic
postulates, our definition of the formula of *Shih Ching* poetry permits
concessions. The interjection *hsi* in the first stanza of poem 136, for
example, is semantically optional but appears to be of musical
interest.

STANZA 1: 子之湯兮, 宛丘之上兮 · · ·
          tzu chih tang hsi, wan ch'iu chih shang hsi . . .

STANZA 2: 坎其擊鼓, 宛丘之下 · · ·
          k'an ch'i chi ku, wan ch'iu chih hsia . . .

STANZA 3: 坎其擊缶, 宛丘之道 · · ·
          k'an ch'i chi fou, wan ch'iu chih tao . . .

The interjection occurring at the end of the second verse of stanza 1
is to agree metrically with the one at the end of the first verse.
We have no doubt here, because the system "*wan ch'iu chih* X" is
not confined to poem 136 (if so, it would pertain more to incremental repetition of the ballad than formula). The fourth item of

[7]The group of words in poem 251 is taken as a verse by Chih Yü (摯虞),
Wen-chang liu-pieh lun (文章流別論), reprint (Taipei, 1960), Vol. II, p. 261,
but refuted by K'ung, *Mao-shih cheng-yi*, and others on the ground that a
lengthy verse does not befit musical postulates. Hao Ching, *Mao-shih yüan-
chieh*, nevertheless, bypasses K'ung's arguments and presents the citation
from poem 271 as another example of the nine-word verse.

[8]*Mao-shih cheng-yün* (毛詩正韻), II, 9a.

the particular system appears in poem 137: *wan ch'iu chih hsü* (栩). A similar instance is the verse *wo hsin shang pei hsi* (我心傷悲兮) in poem 147. The interjection again does not occur to fulfill a semantic requirement but to achieve metrical harmony within the stanza. For the exact expression *wo hsin shang pei* occurs in four other poems (14, 161, 162, 169) without any interjection like the one in 147. Other similar cases where the interjections are optional in our consideration of the semantic formula vary from *ch'i yeh hsü hsi* 其葉湑兮 (214, 218) with relation to *ch'i yeh* X X (reduplicative); *hsi fang chih jen hsi* 西方之人兮 (38) with relation to *hsi jen chih tzu* 西人之子 (203) and *hsi fang mei jen* 西方美人 (38); *nai ju chih jen hsi* 乃如之人兮 (29) with relation to *nai ju chih jen yeh* 乃如之人也 (51); to *ch'ü ch'i ju chih ho* 取妻如之何 (101) with relation to *ch'ü ch'i ju ho* 取妻如何(158).

So far we have considered the flexibility of the formula with special attention to the value of interjections found in classical Chinese poetry. There are still many elements left unnoticed. The reason that we have chosen to rule out interjections in terms of semantics at this early stage is that, except for a few cases in some minor genres, interjections were generally abandoned by Chinese poets in the later eras. True, interjections perfect the metrical quality of *Shih Ching* poetry, by and large; but they do not alter individual semantic indications. Our consideration of a verse, while heeding its musical origin, is inevitably restricted to the elucidation of rhetorical meaning rather than to sheer conjecture about melodious quality. "In literature, as opposed to the sciences," J. B. Hainsworth notes, "the [phrasal] repetition is normally of the matter and not of its arrangement."[9] The interjection *hsi* 兮, for one, does not significantly change the matter as we see it in the case of *wo hsin shang pei* (*hsi*) 我心傷悲 (兮). To an even greater extent, the phrase *yün ho ch'i hsü* 云何其盱 (199) is only another arrangement of *yün ho hsü yi* 云何盱矣 (225), the latter demonstrably a variant of 云何吁矣 (3). Furthermore, *yün ho ch'i yu* 云何其憂 (116) is in the same class, as philological scrutiny has resulted in the recognition that 盱 and 吁 can simply be equated to *yü* 忬 or *yu* 憂.[10]

---

[9] *The Flexibility of the Homeric Formula*, p. 35.

[10] See *Shih Mao-shih-chuan shu*, I, 8b (p. 26); and *Mao-shih chuan-chien t'ung-shih*, II, 12b-13a.

By so classifying the four phrases singled out above we have already confronted the problem of the flexibility of what we call a "formula" generally in the *Shih Ching* context. Because a *Shih Ching* verse is normally comprised of only four words with definitely only four syllables, we confirm a formula most often at the whole-verse level. However, a "repeated word-group" in the concept of Hainsworth's Homeric study can be a succession of any reasonable number of words, with the allowance that variations are mere "accidents." To ascertain our position in the investigation of the *Shih Ching* language and mode of creation, I would call all the following phrases, as grouped in the six following categories, *formulas*:

(a) A verse that repeats itself in several poems: *yu yu wo szu* 悠悠我思 (134, 30, 33, 91); *chi chien chün tzu* 既見君子 (217, 10, 176, 126, 173, 116, 90, 168, 228); *han fei li t'ien* 翰飛戾天 (196, 204).

(b) A verse that repeats itself within one poem: *tseng chih yi shuo yao* 贈之以勺藥 (95); *t'ao t'ao pu kuei* 慆慆不歸 (156). Arguments against the inclusion of such formulas would be that they resemble the refrains of a ballad. But except for a few instances, where the phrases bear the sign of belonging to a chorus, so to speak, to repeat phrases within a single poem remains a device of oral, spontaneous composition by an individual singer. This is also the value of a narrative formula like *Beowulf mapelode* that often serves to open a new paragraph.

(c) A verse that repeats as a whole in the semantic sense but, owing to the general metrical scheme, deviates in length (number of syllables). To this type belong the phrases mentioned above which are disparate only in the addition and omission of interjections: *wo hsin shang pei hsi* 我心傷悲兮 with relation to *wo hsin shang pei* 我心傷悲. Consequently we regard *chih tzu kuei* 之子歸 (22) as a variant of *chih tzu yü kuei* 之子于歸 (9, 6, 12, 28, 156).[11] To a degree, the concession is comparable to Hainsworth's postulate that changes in metrics and elision and corruption in words and word-groups should be counted the same.[12]

[11]I am aware of Parry's warning that to bring out a "play of norm and variation" is "meaningless." See Parry's review of Walter Arend's *Die Typische Scenen bei Homer* (Berlin, 1933) in *Classical Philology*, XXXI (1936), 359. Parry's words are quoted in Donald K. Fry, "Themes and Type-Scenes in *Elene* 1–113," p. 37.

[12]*Flexibility*, p. 36.

(d) Phrases that fluctuate only in their interjections: *nai ju chih jen hsi* 乃如之人兮 (29) with relation to *nai ju chih jen yeh* 乃如之人也 (51). Or adjectival expressions: *ch'i yeh hsü hsü* 其葉滑滑 (119) with relation to *ch'i yeh hsü hsi* 其葉滑兮 (214, 218); and *hui mu ch'i ch'i* 卉木萋萋 (168) to *hui mu ch'i chih* 卉木萋止 (169). A larger dimension of this type is shown in the apparent association of *nü hsin shang pei* 女心傷悲 (154), *nü hsin shang chih* 女心傷止 (169), and *nü hsin pei chih* 女心悲止 (169).

(e) Phrases with words that alternate ideographic elements without changing the basic meaning of the words: *yu hsin yin yin* 憂心慇慇 (257, 192) with relation to 憂心殷殷 (40); *ch'i yeh ching ching* 其葉菁菁 (119) to *chi yeh ch'ing ch'ing* 其葉青青 (225); and *wo kou chih tzu* 我遘之子 (158) to 我覯之子 (214).

(f) Phrases that involve alternative words with the identical meaning: *yu lu yü yü* 麀鹿嗼嗼 (261) with relation to 麀鹿麌麌 (180); *yün ho ch'i hsü* 云何其盱 (199) to *yün ho ch'i yu* 云何其憂 (116); and *shih wo nung jen* 食我農人 (211) to *shih wo nung fu* 食我農夫 (154).

All types of the phrases qualified above remain in the category of the whole-verse formula. They are detected by semantic rather than syntactic principles, although in the consideration of whether inversions and paradigmatic variations are to be allowed, for repetitions of "substantially the same form," we have come across the issue of syntax. The syntactic formulas are termed "formulaic expressions" by Lord, who considers that even only "one word in the same position in the line with other lines or half lines" can qualify the specific line "formulaic."[13] This concept is too generous for the analysis of the *Shih Ching* formulaic language.

Parry's classic definition of the Homeric formula runs: "A group of words which is regularly employed under the same metrical conditions to express a given essential idea."[14] In the definition above and in that of the "formulaic system" Parry stresses similarity of ideas as the primary condition determining any group of words as "formulaic."[15] All in all, the definition is vague, but Lord's emendation makes it even vaguer by adding the term "formulaic

[13]*Singer of Tales*, p. 47.
[14]"Studies in the Epic Technique of Oral Verse-making, I: Homer and Homeric Style," p. 80.
[15]*Ibid.*, p. 85; also see *L'Épithète tradionnelle dans Homère*, pp. 11–15.

expression" on top of it. A formulaic expression, Lord says, is "a line or half-line constructed in the pattern of formulas."[16] He leaves the meaning of "pattern" unexplained: a rhythmical or syntactical pattern? A pattern of ideas?[17] For the sake of clarity, therefore, I discuss the problem of "formulaic expressions" later in this chapter.

On the ground of Parry's thesis, I define the *Shih Ching* formula as follows: A formula is a group of not less than three words forming an articulate semantic unit which repeats, either in a particular poem or several, under similar metrical conditions, to express a given essential idea.

THE WHOLE-VERSE FORMULA

In Parry's definition of the formula, the size of the "group of words" is not clearly limited. Ann Chalmers Watts has studied Parry's many discussions on the matter; she concludes that to Parry, "such necessarily conjunctiveal or introductory expressions as αὐτὰρ ὁ (although he), ὣς ὁ μέν (but thus), etc." are not considered formulaic, although they are "regularly employed under the same metrical conditions to express a given essential idea" in the Homeric poems.[18] She then points out Lord's error in changing his mentor's prudent restrictions upon the length of a formula.[19]

The question whether a brief conjunctival or introductory expression can be justified as formula extends to other fields of oral-formulaic analysis. Magoun's defence that "an element as small and insignificant as *pa* is capable of playing an important role formulaically—and metrically" runs:

> In the case of Anglo-Saxon poetry with its short verses (the structural unit) usually with very complicated metrics, the formulaic character of many single words becomes apparent as *sweordum* (*Jud.* 294b), *to willan* (295a) which not only occur under identical metrical conditions but which

[16]*Singer of Tales*, p. 4.

[17]For a full critical discussion of this question, see Ann Chalmers Watts, *The Lyre and the Harp*, p. 130.

[18]*Ibid.*, p. 70.

[19]*Ibid.*, p. 71. Watts' accusation that Lord has made an unwarranted change of Parry's concept is directed especially against Lord's acceptance as formulaic some "necessarily conjunctival or introductory expressions." She refers us to *The Singer of Tales*, pp. 143, 198, 292–293, and 297–330; and to Lord's "Homer and Other Epic Poetry," in Alan B. Wace and Frank H. Stubbings, eds., *A Companion to Homer* (London, 1962), p. 187.

form obvious portions of A-verses. By the same token the
formulaic character of even shorter, rhetorically less conspicuous words appears clearly as *þa* in *þa reordode* (*And.*
415a), *þa hleoðrode* (537a) where, and doubtless in count-
less other instances, *þa* forms the first measure of a D-
verse. Reversed to *reordode þa, hleoðrode þa* the result is
an E-verse where *þa* fills the second measure.[20]

Whether the size of a formula corresponds to the length of a verse
in a given metrical tradition, we will also have to check against
Chinese poetry. But Magoun's belief is carried on by Creed who,
on several occasions, underlines as formulas those small units like
þa and other auxiliaries, e.g., *scolde, wolde, moste, þence, cuþe,
dorste*.[21] However, in the wake of a criticism advanced by Donald
K. Fry, Creed in 1968 announced his "retreat from the position
. . . that a formula can be as small as a measure," a position he
takes especially in the article "The Making of an Anglo-Saxon
Poem" (1959).[22]

Fry contends that word groups shorter or longer than one
verse (one half-line) in Old English poetry are not formulas.
Because a formula, he assumes, is the product of a system, it must
correspond in length to a system. Fry has demonstrated that the
system in Old English poetry operates only at the level of the half-
line.

In the oral-formulaic analysis, to restrict a formula at the whole-
verse level is conceivably a convenient step to start with, because
the definition of a verse (or in the case of Old English poetry, a half-
line) is comparatively easy to obtain. Hence, according to his
original definition of a whole-verse formula, Creed finds 19.2
percent of the whole-verses in *Boewulf* formulaic.[23]

The percentage of whole-verse formulas in *Beowulf* drops,
however, according to Watts' reconsideration. Watts finds that 1053
whole-verses in *Beowulf* are formulas, or 16.6 percent of the poem.
The figure is not high, especially as 69 of the whole-verse formulas she

[20]"The Theme of the Beasts of Battle in Anglo-Saxon Poetry," pp. 81–82.

[21]See his "Studies in the Techniques of Composition of the Beowulf
Poetry in British Museum MS. Cotton Vitellius A XV," and "The Making
of an Anglo-Saxon Poem."

[22]See the "Additional Remarks" to "The Making," reprinted in Fry
ed., *The Beowulf Poet: A Collection of Critical Essays* (Englewood Cliffs, N.J.,
1968), pp. 141–153. The announcement of retreat appears on p. 153. For
Fry's criticism see "Old English Formulas and Systems," pp. 193–204.

[23]"Studies," p. 390.

TABLE 3:
WHOLE-VERSE FORMULAS IN *Beowulf*

Verse-Type	Number of Verses	Number of Formulas	Percentage of Type
A	2851	666	23.3
B	1047	118	11.4
C	1118	187	16.7
D	853	207	24.4
E	446	45	10.1

counts contain proper names.[24] According to the same principle, she finds that 392 whole-verses or 14.8 percent of *Elene* are formulas.

In the hope of proving his assumption that formulaic poetry involves literary hands, Benson counts 250 whole-verse formulas out of the 3500-verse (1750-line) *Meters of Boethius*. The result supplements Diamond's finding that 1037 out of 5194 verses (2958 lines) are whole-verse formulas in the Cynewulfian group. That is, approximately 20 percent of the *Meters* and 19.9 percent of Cynewulf's verses are whole-verse formulas.[25] Despite the individual researchers' different criteria for collecting data, Creed, Watts, Benson, and Diamond each feels that the poem of his (her) particular concern is by and large formulaic. Formulaic as they all are, Creed's and Watts' conclusion is that *Beowulf* is "oral"; Benson and Diamond stress the possibility that some written (literate) elements are incorporated in the *Meters of Boethius* and, of course, the poems of Cynewulf. The confusion of Old English scholarship with special regard to oral-formulaic analysis appears therein. Duggan cites a casual remark of Lord: "we can conclude that a pattern of 50 or 60 percent formula or formulaic, with 10 to perhaps 25 percent straight formula, indicates clearly literary or written composition."[26] Starting with the statement, Duggan writes about the narrative poem, Old French in particular:

> I would be more specific about the threshold and say that, in general, if [it] is less than 20 per cent straight repetition, it probably derives from literary, or written,

[24]*Lyre and the Harp*, p. 228; also see p. 127.

[25]For Benson's study see "The Literary Character of Anglo-Saxon Formulaic Poetry;" for Diamond's see "The Diction of the Signed Poems of Cynewulf."

[26]Duggan, *The Song of Roland*, p. 29.

creation. When the formula density exceeds 20 percent, it is strong evidence of oral composition.[27]

But how can *Beowulf* be termed oral with only 19.2 percent (Creed's statistics) or 16.6 percent (Watts' statistics) whole-verse (half-line) formulas, while the *Meters of Boethius* with approximately 20 percent and Cynewulf's poems with 19.9 percent whole-verse (half-line) formulas be termed literary or written? Creed, Watts, Benson, and Diamond all take the Anglo-Saxon Poetic Records as the referent in common.[28] None of the poems they deal with crosses the threshold set by Duggan. Shall we say, then, that *Beowulf* is derived from "literary, or written creation," as are the *Meters* and the Cynewulfian poems?

Perhaps "oral or not" is not the matter that really concerns us. Formulaic composition, perhaps, as Benson finds, was once practiced by writing as well as improvising poets. The mode of creation that concerns us is not necessarily oral-formulaic composition, but formulaic composition. Let us see what our Chinese materials reveal concerning this problem.

TABLE 4:
FORMULAIC ANALYSIS OF *Shih Ching*

Section	Number of Verses	Whole-verse Formulas	Percentage of Section
Feng	2608	694	26.6
H.Ya	2326	532	22.8
T.Ya	1616	209	12.9
Sung	734	96	13.1

The total number of verses in *Shih Ching* is 7284, and the total of whole-verses which are formulas accounts for 1531, or 21 percent of the corpus. This figure just passes the threshold of "oral composition" established by Duggan with Old French poetry particularly in view. The percentage considerably increases if verses containing syntactic variants are taken into account. In table 4 I have excluded phrases with variants, no matter how minor they are. Of the phrases in the six categories which I have qualified as formulaic (see the previous section), only those of the first two

[27]*Ibid.*
[28]See Creed, "Studies;" Watts, *The Lyre and the Harp*; Benson, "The Literary Character;" and Diamond, "Signed Poems of Cynewulf."

(phrases with exact repetitions within and without an individual poem) are calculated. It is definite that the numerical figure of whole-verse formulas will amount to approximately 30 percent of the corpus under either of the following conditions: that all the comparable allowances proposed by Hainsworth in the justification of the Homeric formula are permitted in our area;[29] or that all the phrases with comparable syntactic and grammatical variants taken into account by Watts are included in our calculation of the whole-verse formulas.[30] Under either of these conditions, the percentage of the *Shih Ching* whole-verse formulas will be double that of the Old English.

The threshold assumption, when too strict, is always hazardous because no critical criterion can govern materials of various poetic—or metrical—traditions. "Just as the hexameter is the basis of most Homeric formulas, so is the single verse that of Old-Germanic poetry," says Magoun in his seminal writing on the oral-formulaic character of Anglo-Saxon narrative poetry.[31] By whole-verse formula, we mean in the *Shih Ching* exactly the "formula which is co-extensive with a whole poetic line."[32] Though the threshold of Duggan may appear unfair to the Old English researcher, it does not prevent the *Shih Ching* verses from entering the realm of orality. It is up to us whether to let *Shih Ching* be so labeled.

Table 4 shows that 26.6 percent of the verses of the *Feng* section and 22.8 percent of the *H.Ya* section are whole-verse formulas. Are all the poems grouped in these two sections necessarily oral improvisations? At least two in the *H.Ya* are self-evident literate creations somewhat resembling the signed poems of Cynewulf. The poet calls himself Chia-fu in poem 191, and Meng-tzu in poem 200. These poems are fairly formulaic but apparently not improvisational products. Two other poems bearing their poet's name, Chi-fu, fall in the section of *T.Ya,* which according to our statistics is the lowest in percentage of whole-verse formulas. However, the formula densities in these apparently literate compositions (259, 260) are similar to poems 191 and 200 in the *H.Ya* section.

[29]*Flexibility*, p. 36.
[30]*The Lyre and the Harp.* See esp. Appendix B, pp. 227–265.
[31]"Oral-Formulaic Character of Anglo-Saxon Narrative Poetry," p. 106.
[32]Parry thinks that this is "the easiest formula for the poet to handle." See "Whole Formulaic Verses in Greek and Southslavic Heroic Poetry," p. 194.

Further, the four literate compositions altogether are not necessarily less formulaic than other poems which we could on account of internal evidence call "oral."

The poems of the *Sung* section are relatively less formulaic than those of other sections. So grouped, they appear to be at the average of the *T.Ya*, but a close investigation uncovers the *Sung* as an extremely divergent section.

TABLE 5:
FORMULAIC ANALYSIS OF THE *Sung*.

House	Number of Verses	Whole-Verse Formulas	Percentage of Formulas in House
Chou	337	51	15.1
Lu	243	41	16.8
Shang	154	4	2.6

Some scholars argue that the *Chou sung*, being oldest, suffered greatest textual damage and has become fragmented in its present form.[33] Nevertheless, the poems of the Chou and Lu royal houses fall between the poems of the *T.Ya* (12.9 percent) and the *H.Ya* (22.8 percent) sections in the degree to which they are formulaic. And the Shang group (five poems altogether) is the least formulaic of the whole corpus of *Shih Ching*. Also, two of the four whole-verse formulas in the Shang group are related to the *T.Ya* (poem 264) and the *H.Ya* (poem 178). In other words, within its own category only two verse-lines recur. Practically every line is patterned anew, a rare phenomenon in ancient poetry.

Refrains and incremental repetitions are thought to be some of the significant compositional features of the ballad. Table 6 is prepared in the interest of reconsidering the nature of the *Shih Ching* poems traditionally categorized as *feng, ya,* and *sung.*

Table 6 and table 5 reveal, first of all, that the *Feng* poems which for generations have been regarded as the folk ballads of the anthology, are not the densest in "refrains" or "incremental repetitions" among the various groups. The section of *Feng* comes third, following the groups of Lu verses and the *H.Ya.* Again, the result questions the validity of Dobson's theory that stylistically as

[33]Cf. Fu Szu-nien, *"Chou sung shuo,"* in his *chi.*

TABLE 6:
RECURRENCES WITHIN SECTION OR GROUP

Section or Group	Number of Verses	Whole-Verse Repetitions in Group	Percentage of Group
Feng	2608	282	10.8
H.Ya	2326	271	11.6
T.Ya	1616	111	6.8
Chou S.	337	7	2.07
Lu S.	243	29	11.9
Shang S.	154	2	1.3

well as linguistically the development of early Chinese prosody shows a series of what he calls "successive stages": that the *Feng* was derived from the *H.Ya*, the *H.Ya* from the *T.Ya*, and the *T.Ya* from the *Sung*.[34]

The data presented in tables 4 and 5, furthermore, reveal that the liturgic hymns of the Shang are far removed from those of the Chou and Lu stylistically, although the three are traditionally classed as a trinity. This fact contributes to verifying the widely accepted dating of the Shang verses as later compositions belonging to the Duchy of Sung. In terms of the whole-verse formulas with reference to the whole corpus, the Lu group is close to the Chou, both standing between the *T.Ya* and *H.Ya*. However, in terms of the whole-verse recurrences within the individual groups the Lu rises significantly to the highest, whereas the Chou drops considerably low, superior only to the Shang group. I regard this mobility as evidence that the Chou hymns are much earlier works than the Lu. The increase of repeated phrases within a group, as shown in the Lu verses, may indicate the demise of a seminal style: that of the Chou liturgics, if the extant texts are enough evidence. The decisive period of the Lu composition with the name of a known author, Hsi Szu (奚斯), has been proved to be quite late— so that the verses should share the manifest style of the *H.Ya* and *Feng* instead of the slow, solemn mood of the Chou hymns.

Meanwhile, that the poets of the *Feng* and *H.Ya* were exposed to the language of the Chou hymns is conceivable, although these poets seem to have rejected the style peculiar to the liturgic mood

[34]"Origin and Development of Prosody in Early Chinese Poetry."

TABLE 7:
FORMULAS PARTICULAR TO SECTION OR GROUP

Section or Group	Number of Formulas	Formulas Particular to Group	Percentage of Formulas Particular to Group
Feng	694	42	6.05
H.Ya	532	55	10.3
T.Ya	209	23	11.0
Chou S.	51	10	19.6
Lu S.	41	0	0
Shang S.	—	—	—

of the Chou court. Of the 51 whole-verse formulas detected in the Chou group, 10 are not shared by other groups.

Table 7 shows that the *Chou sung* is highest in percentage of whole-verse formulas not known—or utilized—by poets of other areas.[35] This indicates the isolated or lofty position of the particular group. A comparison of the figures overall shows that the lower the percentage of formulas particular to a group, the more "vernacular" or "oral" the verses therein are. As far as popularity is concerned the verses of Lu, though categorized in the hymnal area, fall back rather to other groups than to the *Chou sung*. This shows how internal evidence contributes to ascertaining assumptions frequently made on the basis of external evidence.

FORMULAIC EXPRESSIONS

To calculate the whole-verse formulas by percentage, with the corpus taken as the referent, is certainly one of the reliable methods of determining whether the given material is so formulaic as to fit the specific type of literary analysis. It is, however, only one of the methods. Formulas fall into two divisions. The whole-verse formulas, as we have defined them on the preceding pages, are what the oral formulaic analysts call "semantic formulas." The other type of formula is called "syntactic formula" by some scholars and "formulaic expression" by Lord.

[35]The figure of whole-verse formulas of the Shang group is not included in table 7 for consideration, as it is too small. A group of 154 lines with only 4 or 2.6 percent whole-verse formulas (see table 5) does not merit further consideration in this table.

The definition Lord specifies for "formulaic expression" is far from clear. Lord says cryptically: "By formulaic expression I denote a line or half line constructed on the pattern of the formulas."[36] But in *The Singer of Tales,* we find that by "pattern" Lord means a rhythmical-syntactical, not a semantical, formation.[37] Lord, noting the singer's "instinctive grasp" of specific words or word-groups, emphasizes the decisive role of rhythm in the process of improvisation. "One word begins to suggest another by its very sound," he observes, "one phrase suggests another not only by reason of idea or by a special ordering of ideas, but also by acoustic value."[38] From the examples Lord cites in his thesis we know that by "formulaic expression" he means a formulaic system plus other traits of oral literature including, perhaps, the cluster of formulas.[39] In this investigation I intend to meet as many features of formulaic expressions as I can uncover in the *Shih Ching* anthology.

A system in *Shih Ching* poetry may be defined as follows: a group of verses, usually loosely related metrically and semantically, which are related in form by the identical relative placement of two elements, one a constant compound of words, and the other a variable word or word-group usually fulfilling the rhyming pattern.

The diagram below shows how some phrases can be systematized to illustrate our definition:

之子于 ——
　　　垣 (181/2)
　　　歸 (9/2,3), (12/1,2,3), (6/1,2,3), (28/1,2,3), (156/4)
　　　釣 (226/3)
　　　狩 (226/3)
　　　征 (179/8), (181/1)
　　　苗 (179/3)
　　　歸 (22/1,2,3)
無 ——
　　　裳 (63/1)
　　　帶 (63/2)
　　　服 (63/3)
　　　良 (229/7)

---

[36]*Singer of Tales,* p. 4.
[37]See p. 36, 41, 44, 47, *et passim.* Also cf. Watts, *Lyre and the Harp,* pp. 130–132.
[38]*Singer of Tales,* p. 33.
[39]*Ibid.,* p. 60.

The whole system originates in the constant compound *chih tzu* 之子, a formulaic expression in its own right, transformed from the "genitive" case. We may call the compound "genitive absolute" in view of its original grammatic relation to *pi ch'i chih tzu* 彼其之子 (68, 80, 108, 117, 151), *pi liu chih tzu* 彼留之子 (74), *pi sung chih tzu* 必宋之子 (138), and the like. The first six words in our diagram following the expression *chih tzu yü* 之子于 are the variables that also fulfill the individual rhyming patterns.[40] The seventh instance where *yü* 于 is absent is explained by the fact that a singer is bound to seek phrases "by analogy with other phrases" in the general acoustic pattern. Poem 22 is fundamentally constructed in the pattern of three-word verse; the singer, accordingly, drops the superfluous *yü* in the course of verse-making. The rest of the entries (among which, by the way, *wu* 無 forms a subsystem) are alike in the observation of metrical principles.

The rhyming element of *Shih Ching* poetry does not necessarily come at the end of a verse, especially when the ending syllable is an interjectional particle. In assuming a system, therefore, one has to allow the "constant compound of words" to be flexible, sometimes clinging together and sometimes separated by the variable word or word-group. For example:

Or in the pattern:

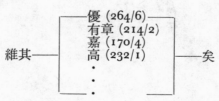

Also noteworthy is the system that, in the absence of interjectional particles, involves constant words clearly separated by variable rhyming elements of absolute semantic value.

[40]Cf. *Mao-shih cheng-yün.*

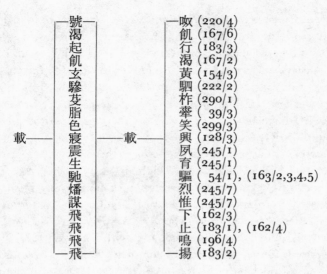

Loosely applied, there are many other verses which we may categorize within the foregoing system. Phrases like *tsai ch'ü po po* 載驅薄薄(105), *tsai huo chi chi* 載穫濟濟(290) and *tsai chou ch'in ch'in* 載驟駸駸(162) are formulaic at least at the level of Gestalt in terms of the generative view proposed by Nagler.[41] And some of the entries in the diagram are doubtless whole-verse formulas. This may support Donald K. Fry's argument that a formula is "the product of a system," and "of exactly the same size as that system."[42] The "systemic origin" view of formula virtually parallels the "generative" view.

Groups of formulaic verses which frequently occur together are termed "clusters of formulas" by Lord and are supposed to be one of the characteristic signs of oral style.[43] The recurrence of clusters of formulas (which allow various changes, such as inversions and separations of systemic elements) is also one of the salient stylistic features of *Shih Ching*. The verses of the second half of poem 168 cited in Chapter One, for example, are groups of simultaneously recurrent phrases. In such cases, it seems evident that the singer does not really depend upon mnemonics more than he does on the technique of phrasal analogy. The ability to create phrases by a-

[41]"Towards a generative View."
[42]"Old English Formulas and Systems," p. 204.
[43]*Singer of Tales*, p. 58ff.

nalogy in a particular acoustic pattern is believed by oral-formulaic scholars to be the ultimate a singer obtains. Here again the generative view and the systemic-origin theory of the formula meet. Large-scale clusters of formulas occur not only in poem 168, but in many other poems scattered throughout *Shih Ching,* such as poems 121 (*Feng*) and 162 (*H.Ya*). The phenomenon has come to be associated more with the technique of compositoin by themes than simply with the building of lyrical lines.

Sometimes new phrases emerge through the clustering of formulas. By reflex the singer is able to "originate" a vivid expression that often seems to belong to another system. The meaning of the new expression, furthermore, is sometimes significantly removed from the formulas it derives from .The verse *han fei li t'ien* 翰飛戾天, for instance, is a formula (poems 196, 204) with which are associated a number of verses identifiable as a common system. In poem 204, in the same stanza where the formula occurs, we also find the verse *ch'ien t'ao yü yüan* 潛逃于淵, a verse built upon another system. The stanza goes:

(7) 匪鶉匪鳶，翰飛戾天； *fei ch'un fei yüan, han fei li t'ien*;
　　匪鱣匪鮪，潛逃于淵。*fei shan fei wei, ch'ien t'ao yü yüan.*　27–28

(7) Neither [am I] an eagle, a falcon,　　　　　　　　　　　　25
　　That can flap and soar up to heaven;
　　Nor [am I] a sturgeon, a snout-fish,
　　That can plunge to hide in the deep.

And two lines in poem 239 run:

(3) 鳶飛戾天，魚躍于淵。*yüan fei li t'ien, yü yao yü yüan.*　　9–10

(3) The falcon soars up to heaven;
　　The fish plunges in the deep.　　　　　　　　　　　　　　10

Though it might be erroneous to insist that the lines of poem 239 are absolutely derived from the cited stanza of poem 204, the two verses from poem 239 appear to be a condensation of the four verses from the other. This condensation is syntactic only, for semantically the verses of the second citation differ much from those of the first. Although created on the same system producing the lines in the first citation, "*yüan fei li t'ien, yü yao yü yüan*" is metaphorically free from all the pejorative color that blackens the mood of poem 204, a trooper's complaint.[44]

In an attempt to explicate a single term that recurs in both the *Feng* and *H.Ya*, Wen I-to commits himself to the assumption that the verses of the *Feng* precede those of the *H.Ya*. He suggests that wherever the connotation of an idiom in the *H.Ya* appears not to be consistent with its use in the *Feng*, the meaning specified for the *H.Ya* verse is a derivative. The *Feng* defines the "original meaning" of an idiom, he implies.[45] Wen's contention that, contrarily, the *H.Ya* precedes the *Feng*, is as vain as Dobson's.[46] My position is that the poems of those two sections were mostly contemporaneous, and influences were reciprocal. One is not justified in assuming that the *Feng* precedes the *H.Ya*, or the contrary. By approaching the problem through analysis of formulaic expressions recurrent in both, we may perhaps realize the subtle interplay at times taking place among those poems.

An important cluster of formulas in *Shih Ching* includes a formula about the spring days drawing out, another about the oriole in tune, and a third about aster-gathering "in abundance" *(ts'ai fan ch'i ch'i)*. This cluster of formulas occurs at least twice in the classical anthology, once in the *Feng* section (154) and again in the *H.Ya* (168), in different order of lines—as Lord in *The Singer of Tales* predicts how a cluster of formulas can occur.[47] In another *Feng* poem (13) the cluster is gracefully broken. Only the aster-gathering motif is utilized, in company with the leitmotif of "return":

(1) 于以采蘩：于沼于沚。*yü yi ts'ai fan, yü chao yü chih.*
于以用之：公侯之事。*yü yi yung chih: kung hou chih shih.*   3–4

(2) 于以采蘩：于澗之中。*yü yi ts'ai fan, yü chien chih chung.*
于以用之：公侯之宮。*yü yi yung chih: kung hou chih kung.*   7–8

---

[44]The shift of meanings on the basis of almost identical metaphor has caused numerous problems to the *Shih Ching* annotators. Ch'en Huan, for one, is troubled; see his *Shih Mao-shih-chuan shu*, XX, 8a, and XXIII, 16a. Arthur Waley compromises by naming the bird of poem 239 "kite" and the waters "pool," so as to remove the dangerous, unfathomable connotations of the "falcon" and the "deep" which he apparently thinks fit poem 204.

[45]"*K'uang-chai ch'ih-tu*" (匡齋尺牘), *ch'üan-chi*, Vol I, p. 366.

[46]"Origin and Development of Prosody in Early Chinese Poetry," p. 248.

[47]p. 58.

(3) 被之僮僮，夙夜在公；*pei chih t'ung t'ung, su yeh tsai kung;*
被之祁祁，薄言還歸。*pei chih ch'i ch'i, po yen huan kuei.*   11–12

(1) See, she gathers white aster
By the pools, on the little islands.
See, she uses it
At the rituals of her prince and lord.

(2) See, she gathers white aster   5
Down in the ravine.
See, she uses it
In the ancestral hall of prince and lord.

(3) Her tall wig nods
At dawn of (*sic*) night, while she plies her task   10
With tall wig gently swaying
Here she comes back to her room.
                              (Waley's translation)

I have chosen this translation for the purpose of showing how the
formula *ts'ai fan ch'i ch'i* can pass unnoticed by even a disciplined
Sinologist like Arthur Waley.[48] The emergence of *ch'i ch'i* toward
the end of the poem is predetermined at the Gestalt level by the
motif of *ts'ai fan*. Waley, following the traditional Chinese commentary, takes *ch'i ch'i* as qualifying the woman's "tall wig" (*pei*
被), and renders the idiom as "gently swaying," completely
depriving it of its meaning, which is established in poems 154 and
168.

My objection to Waley's interpretation is that it does not heed
the leitmotif of return, which is a substantial theme in all poems of
aster-gathering in *Shih Ching*. The poem is a manifestation of the
mentioned cluster of formulas: it is an amplified version of the
specific aster-gathering motif. The cluster, in whatever order, expresses a desire to return. And the particular formula is dyed with
the sorrow of being prevented from realizing that wish. Taking the
adjectival duplicative as generated by the initial motif of aster-
gathering, we have no justification for interpreting it as "gently
swaying" to modify the "tall wig," as Waley puts it in accordance
with the orthodox commentary.[49] We regard the *Shih Ching* poem,

[48] *The Book of Songs*, p. 90.
[49] Cf. Ma Jui-ch'en, *Mao-shih chuan-chien t'ung-shih*, III, 4a; and Fang
Yü-jun, *Shih Ching yüan shih*, II, 4a–5b.

in general, as formulaic composition and its phrases as normally originating in a formulaic system. Therefore, *ch'i ch'i* has to remain in connotation where its equivalent means at the higher level as determined by the cluster of formulas. I suggest that the correct rendering of the last two verses of poem 13 is: "Carrying them (asters) in abundance, here returns [the gatherer]."

This poem, finally, embodies most of the significant characteristics Lord attributes to formulaic composition. Lord notes that "conjunction-verb" is frequent "in a style in which actions or things are added one to another in series."[50] The verbal force of the initial *yü* 于 stands out as the best illustration of this phenomenon. Besides, the "adding style," a term Parry invents to denote the oral style of composition in which "necessary enjambement" is absent, and pleonasm, which is also common in oral poetry, are simply too obvious in this poem, and in *Shih Ching* in general, to call for lengthy discussion.[51]

[50]*Singer of Tales*, p. 41ff.
[51]*Ibid.*; for "adding style" and its relation to the absence of enjambement, see pp. 54–55; for the problem of pleonasm, see pp. 34–35.

THREE

The Formula: II

There are normally three ways to demonstrate the formulaic character of a poem. The tabulation of whole-verse formulas followed by a statistic comparison, shown in the preceding chapter, is good for both long and short compositions. For the narrative poem of considerable length, the traditional way of manifesting the density of formulaic phrases is by selecting (preferably at random) a group of about twenty-five lines and putting a solid line beneath the word-groups which are found elsewhere in the poem unchanged and a broken line under those which are of the same pattern as others. Parry believes this is "the easiest and best way."[1] Robert C. Culley, however, in dealing with the biblical psalms, chooses to avoid it and approaches the problem with another plan: he first lists the primary phrases which conform to his definition of the formula and then shows how these phrases are distributed among the psalms.[2] Culley's implicit rationale is that lyrical psalms deserve a special treatment different from that designed for narrative epics.[3] I feel that the methodology of Parry is largely adoptable for the consideration of

[1]This is the classic approach proposed and practiced by Milman Parry in "Studies in the Epic Technique of Oral Verse-making, I: Homer and Homeric Style," pp. 118–121. Ever since then (1930), researchers of the Homeric and Old English oral-formulaic compositions have found it convenient to follow. Hence, Albert B. Lord in *The Singer of Tales*; Francis P. Magoun, Jr. in the "Oral-Formulaic Character of Anglo-Saxon Narrative Poetry;" Robert P. Creed, in the "Studies in the Techniques of Composition of the Beowulf Poetry in British Museum MS. Cotton Vitellius A XV," and practically all others mentioned hitherto in the present study.

[2]See *Oral Formulaic Language in the Biblical Psalms*, pp. 28–101. In a broader sense, Ann Chalmers Watts also utilizes this method in her exhaustive listing of the formulas in *Beowulf* and *Elene*; see *The Lyre and the Harp*, pp. 226–265.

[3]Cf. *Biblical Psalms*, pp. 28–31.

lyrical as well as epic poetry. The following pages present the *Shih Ching* formulas and formulaic expressions through the approach that Parry and other scholars of oral-formulaic epics have verified. I believe that insofar as their mode of creation is identical, literary products of different origins come to disclose themselves in a common light. By the "mode of creation" I refer to the mode of composition by formulas and themes. As a supplement to this way of presentation, I have prepared a listing of sample formulas and formulaic expressions in a way resembling that of Culley and Watts.[4]

Except for one, the sample poems subjected to analysis below are selected at random: *at random* in the sense that until each is accordingly underlined I have no way of telling exactly its degree of formulaicness. In order to have a good variety of materials, I have chosen a poem from approximately every fifty numbers in the anthology: the array of poems—54, 101, 168, 204, 252, 301— come two from the *Feng* section, another two from the *H.Ya*, one from the *T.Ya*, and another one from the *Sung*. The distribution conforms to the proportion of the number of poems in each section. With the exception of poem 252 (Chart V), every poem is treated in full; this is done in the interest of discussing the aesthetic implications of each. The total of lines (full verses) subjected to scrutiny is 208, roughly 3 percent of the corpus.

CHART I: 54 (*Tsai chih* 載馳)

(1) 載馳載驅，歸唁衛侯； *tsai ch'ih tsai ch'ü, kuei yen wei hou;*
　　驅馬悠悠，言至于漕。 *ch'ü ma yu yu, yen chih yü ts'ao.*
　　大夫跋涉，我心則憂。 *ta fu pa she, wo hsin tse yu.* 5–6

(2) 既不我嘉，不能旋反。 *chi pu wo chia, pu neng hsüan fan.*
　　視爾不臧，我思不遠。 *shih erh pu tsang, wo szu pu yüan.* 9–10

(3) 既不我嘉，不能旋濟。 *chi pu wo chia, pu neng hsüan chi.*
　　視爾不臧，我思不閟。 *shih erh pu tsang, wo szu pu pi.* 13–14

(4) 陟彼阿丘，言采其蝱。 *chih pi o ch'iu, yen ts'ai ch'i meng.*
　　女子善懷，亦各有行； *nü tzu shan huai, yi ko yu hsing;*
　　許人尤之，衆穉且狂！ *hsü jen yu chih, chung chih ch'ieh k'uang!* 19–20

[4]See Appendix B.

(5) 我行其野，芃芃其麥。 *wo hsing ch'i yeh, p'eng p'eng ch'i mai.*
控于大邦，誰因誰極？ *k'ung yü ta pang, shui yin shui chi?*
大夫君子，無我有尤； *ta fu chün tzu, wu wo yu yu:*
百爾所思，不如我所之！ *pai erh so szu, pu ju wo so chih!*   27–28

(1) Let me gallop let me go
    To share the Lord of Wei, my brother's woe!
    I urge my horse on the long road
    Till I should halt at Ts'ao!
    A deputy has journeyed over the grassland and streams;
    My heart remains stricken with grief.

(2) You have denied my wish to travel;
    I cannot go back like that.
    And you think my plan baleful;
    I have no way of relieving my sorrow.   10

(3) You have denied my wish to travel;
    I cannot go back across the river.
    And you think my plan baleful;
    I have no way of stopping my thoughts.

(4) I climb the sloping hill,
    To pick the toad-lilies.
    Thoughts abound in a woman like me,
    Sure can find her right way to follow.
    The people of Hsü blame my intent;
    Childish, these people are so presumptuous!   20

(5) I walk into the fields
    Where the grains are thick and rich.
    To a great land I would plead for aid,
    But to which shall I go, on whom can I rely?
    O you great officers, nobles,
    Don't lay blame on me:
    The thoughts of all the hundred of you,
    None can really match my single proposal!

Supporting Evidence

   (1) 163/2,3,4,5. Also cf. 105/1; 128/3; 154/3; 162/3; 162/4;

183/1; 162/5; 167/6; 176/4; 183/2; 192/9; 196/4; 204/5; 220/4; 222/2; 245/1; 245/7; 290; 299; 115/1, 254/8.

(2) Cf. the phonetically similar 言歸 (*ngiăn:*ngian); 2/3; 13/3; 168/6; 187/1,2,3; 188/2; 226/1; 298/2.

(3) Cf. 39/4; 227/1; 299/2.

(6) 14/1,2,3; 168/5; 176/2; 176/4. Also cf. 14/3; 162/1; 167/6; 169/2; 28/3; 33/2; 229/4,6; 65/1,2,3; 146/2; 192/1; 196/1; 197/2; 147/2,3; 156/1; 159/4; 203/2; 223/8; 225/2,3; 256/11; 258/5.

(7) 54/3. Also cf. 29/1,2; 59/1; 73/1,2; 89/2; 146/1,2,3; 60/1,2; 87/1,2; 89/2; 188/1,2; 192/7; 199/2; 199/7; 257/3; 258/ 3,4,5,6; 264/1.

(8) 54/3.

(9) 54/3. Also cf. 137/3; 256/11; 33/4; 193/2; 195/2.

(10) 54/3. Also cf. 35/3; 197/8; 167/3; 191/9; 225/2; 257/4.

(11) 54/2, etc. (See *supporting evidence* for line 7.)

(12) 54/2.

(13) 54/2. etc. (See *supporting evidence* for line 9.)

(14) 54/2, etc. (See *supporting evidence* for line 10.)

(15) Cf. 3/2,3; 218/4; 241/6; 14/2,3; 169/3; 205/1; 305/6.

(16) 14/2,3; 108/1,2,3; 169/3; 205/1; 188/2,3; 222/2. Also cf. 8/1,2,3; 9/2,3; 154/4; 182/3; 222/2; 299/1; 209/1; 226/3; 256/10.

(15–16) Cf. the recurrent cluster of formulaic expressions *chih pi...yen ts'ai* 陟彼...言采: 205/1; 218/4; 14/2,3.

(17–18) Contracted formula *nü tzu yu hsing* 女子有行: 39/2; 51/1,2; 59/2.

(19) Cf. 107/1; 141/1; 153/4; 189/7; 190/4; 198/4.

(21) 188/1,2,3.

(22) Cf. the system "adjectival reduplicative 其 subject": 6/1; 30/4; 33/1; 35/3; 44/1,2; 181/1; 189/5; 274; 290.

(25) 258/8.

(25–27) Cf. 33/4 and the contracted formula *fan pai chün tzu* 凡百君子: 194/3,4; 200/7.

(28) 119/1,2.

The poem is grouped in the Yung (鄘) of the *Feng* section, numbered 54 in the Mao text. In view of an entry in *Tso Chuan* (左傳), commentators have unanimously taken it as a lament of Dame Mu of Hsü (許穆夫人).[5] In his admirable rendering, Ezra Pound subtitles the poem: "Baroness Mu impeded in her wish to help famine victims in Wei."[6] Arthur Waley also surrenders to the traditional interpretation, but he thinks that by "a great land" (line 23) the speaker implies Hsü, which is a small state, "out of conventional courtesy"—this is a mistake.[7] Dame Mu is a princess of Wei (衞) married to the Lord of Hsü; upon hearing of the catastrophe of her brother's court, she attempts to ride back to condole with him, but her husband orders her to stay. Mourning, according to *Tso Chuan*, she makes the poem. To an extent, the credibility of the poem's authorship is comparable with that of the so-called Caedmonian hymn singled out by Magoun in his article about the "Anglo-Saxon oral singer."[8] Both poems, while bearing little internal evidence, are identified as attributable to particular makers by historians, and both are highly formulaic in language.

A glance at the chart shows that approximately 80 percent of the verses are formulaic, including clusters of formulaic expressions and lines showing the mobility of some *Shih Ching* formulas, which at one time are contracted and at another expanded. The supporting evidence tells its own story articulately. However, some aspects of the formulaic style are complicated, and these call for further consideration.

A preverbal Gestalt "generating a family of allomorphs" can be the conceptual framework for the formula in this type of composition.[9] The first stanza of poem 54 contains an example which illustrates Nagler's supposition. Conceivably, the expressions of lines 3 and 6 generate each other reciprocally constructing the flexible formula *wo hsin yu yu* 我心悠悠 (39/4) or *yu yu wo hsin* 悠悠我心 (91/1). This is especially conspicuous when we bring in poem 39 for comparison. Poem 39 tells of a woman's yearning to

[5]閔二年傳: 許穆夫人賦載馳. *Ch'un Ch'iu san chuan* (春秋三傳) reprint (Taipei, 1962), p. 147.

[6]*The Confucian Odes*, p. 25.

[7]See *The Book of Songs*, p. 95. Waley apparently misreads the meaning of *k'ung* in line 23. For correct scrutiny of the word, see Ch'en Huan, *Shih Mao-shih-chuan shu*, V. 12a-12b (pp. 145–150); also as supplements, Li Ch'ao-sun (李超孫), *Shih shih tsu k'ao* (詩氏族考), p. 20; and Fu Szu-nien, *"Ta-tung hsiao-tung shuo"* (大東小東說), in his *chi*, Vol. VI, pp. 3–4.

[8]"Bede's Story of Caedmon: the Case History of an Anglo-Saxon Oral Singer."

[9]Cf. Nagler, "Towards a Generative View of the Oral Formula."

return to Wei (where the heroine of poem 54 also craves to go) to visit her kinsmen. The last four lines are:

(4) 思須與漕，我心悠悠；*szu hsü yü ts'ao, wo hsin yu yu*;
　　駕言出遊，以寫我憂。*chia yen ch'u yu, yi hsieh wo yu.*　　　23–24

(4) Thinking of Hsü and Ts'ao,
　　Long my heart yearns;
　　I will harness and drive out,
　　To release my grief.　　　　　　　　　　　　　　24

Many key words in the passage, including the name of a place, resurface in various positions in poem 54. Line 3 of the latter is to a degree a contraction of lines 22 and 23 of poem 39. The reduplicative changes to qualify, instead of "my heart," the action of harness-driving. Both passages, as if out of a common grinder, halt with the attention to *wo yu*. The decisive reason that the formulaic expression occurs in two poems of different groups (*Pei* versus *Yung*) is doubtless the naming of the place, Ts'ao, which is certain.[10] Ts'ao appears in *Shih Ching* and *Tso Chuan* to be the last surviving castle-town of any importance to the much suffering state of Wei.[11] Here we see that although line 4 is not underlined in the chart, the role this line plays in the composition of the stanza is by no means less significant than others definitely marked as formulas. I assume that in making a poem of this type, every single motif is vigorous enough in its own right to generate lines that are formulaic. And I regard this feature as the primary meaning of composition by type-scene (or theme). This makes understandable why a group of oral-formulaic scholars have recently sensed the ambiguity of the term "formula," for, as they would argue, formulas per se are not materially essential to "composition by formulas."

Stanzas 2 and 3 of poem 54 form a unit, providing an example

[10]For the reasons that both groups (and the Wei 衛) share similar historical and geographical references as well as a common metaphorical system henceforth determined, see K'ung Ying-ta, *Mao-shih cheng-yi*, II-1, 1a-3b; Ch'en Huan, *shu*, III, 1a (p. 75); and Ku Yen-wu, *Jih chih lu*, III, 6–8. Also cf. Fu Szu-nien, *"Chou tung-feng yü Yin yi-min"* (周東封與殷遺民), in his *chi*, Vol. VI, pp. 23–30; and Fu, *"Yi Hsia tung hsi shuo"* (夷夏東西說), *chi*, Vol. VI, pp. 42–43.

[11]The historical account of Wei's suffering from the constant assaults of the Tartars and, finally, its conquest is found in *Tso Chuan*; see note 5. The Duchy of Wei is reported to have succumbed in 660 B.C.

of incremental repetition. To be sure, incremental repetition is not characteristic only of the ballad. Some *Shih Ching* poems are feasibly termed "ballads" on account of the presence of refrains and incremental repetitions.[12] But there are even more which are not ballads in the traditional sense although refrains and repetitions do occur in them. The third stanza repeats to reinforce the speaker's strong intent to return. The definite verb *chi* 濟 replaces *fan* 反, and the adjustment specifies the situation the speaker is in. Geographical information attests that one has to cross rivers to travel from Hsü to Wei, Chu Hsi remarks.[13] So do imagistic precedents: the deputy has ridden over the grass and through the streams. The repetition, therefore, implements the poem's thematic precision rather than just fulfilling postulates of music; the latter are secondarily important in this case.

The subsequent stanza reveals some of the most important poetic motifs in the *Shih Ching* tradition. Packed into only a few lines (15–20) are the climbing of hill and the picking of plants, which illuminate the theme of a wife's lament. The temperament of the stanza, judged in reference to the exclamatory mood that imbues the last two lines directed against the society, is protest. Its overtone, however, is grief rather than fury, and in terms of formulaic analysis, grief rather than fury is the mood normally supported by the motifs of hill-climbing and plant-plucking in *Shih Ching*, especially when the two are simultaneously utilized. Poem 3 of the anthology, where again the notes *ts'ai* 采, *chih* 陟, and *huai* 懷 are crucial, embodies grief while disclaiming excessive woe: "to discontinue my anguish" *wei yi pu yung shang* (維以不永傷). This seems to be a line which Confucius has in mind when he makes his defensive remark for *Shih Ching* poetry: "*Kuan chü* is expressive of enjoyment without being licentious and of grief without being hurtfully excessive" (*Analects* III, 20). Without recourse to poem 3, which includes many formulaic expressions of the same thematic origin, we could be misled by the outcry in line 20 into supposing that desperate fury is the mood underlined.

The catalogue of formulaic expressions, further, clarifies line 17, where the object of *huai* 懷 is not literally specified. In the *Shih Ching*

---

[12]For a fuller account of this subject, see Shih-hsiang Chen, "The *Shih Ching*: Its Generic Significance in Chinese Literary History and Poetics."
[13]*Shih chi-chuan*, III, 12b.

tradition, a "woman's thinking" usually means either her love of the opposite sex (e.g., poems 23, 76) or thoughts of homeland, sometimes alluded to as "kinsman." Four of the five occurrences of this "woman's thinking" expressed in the poems of the Pei-Yung-Wei group are directed either graphically or implicitly toward, instead of the opposite sex, her homeland the Duchy of Wei (poems 33, 39, 51, 54). The catastrophe of Wei conceivably sent many of its women married in foreign lands into this rare tragic situation. The situation could probably only be understood by Hildeburh, the Danish princess married to King Fian of Frisia.[14] Comparing line 17 of poem 54 with other poems where a woman's thinking is mentioned makes it clear that the line from poem 39, *yu huai yü wei* 有懷于衞, summarizes all the implications of a woman's thinking.

Lines 17–18 also feature the highly mobile character of the *Shih Ching* formula. A glance at the two lines tells how closely related they are to an important formula of woman's lamentation, *nü tzu yu hsing*, 女子有行 (39/2; 51/1,2; 59/2). As Milman Parry warns against bringing out a "play of norm and variation" in formulaic analysis,[15] I do not describe either the two lines (17–18) or the definite formula as more original than the other. If we take the former as the "norm," the latter appears to be the expanded version of a formula; if we regard the latter as the norm, the former is best termed a "contracted" or "condensed" version of the other expression. Owing to the fact that neither of the two expressions lacks force, which is evident in the manifold connotations of each, we cannot readily determine which is which as we do in the case of *han fei li t'ien* (see Chapter Two).

A similar problem is found toward the end of the poem: the subtle interaction between lines 25 and 27. This is apparently an interplay of greater dimension than the other in the fourth stanza. The interaction takes place in crossing over the barrier of line 26. I refer to the relation between "*ta fu chün tzu . . . pai erh suo szu*" and the formula *fan pai chün tzu* 凡百君子 (vocative in poems 194 and 200) as well as the expression *pai erh chün tzu* 百爾君子 (33/4). Through the comparison of these lines I have reached the conclu-

---

[14]See "The Fight at Finnsburg" and *Beowulf* 1063–1159a in Fr. Klaeber, ed., *Beowulf and The Fight at Finnsburg,* 3rd ed. (Boston, 1950), pp. 245–249 and 40–44.

[15]Cf. note 12, Chapter Two.

sion that "hundred" in line 27 qualifies "you" but not "thought"—
"the thought of you, hundred great nobles, does not match what I
propose!" I consequently question the validity of Waley's translation of line 27 into "All your many plans."[16]

Lines 15–16 form a cluster of formulas expressing the idea that
grief ought to be discontinued; line 21, which opens the final verse
paragraph, is another formula with the same meaning. This formula
is also utilized three times in poem 188, twice followed by expressions
of the formulaic system patterning line 16. As they are recurrent
lines suggestive of the intention to discontinue present woe—
comparable to the Old English exclamation "*þæs oferode þisses swa
mæg!*"— the intimate relation between line 21 and the cluster of
formulas in lines 15–16 is unmistakable. While the cluster of formulas sets forth the idea of stopping grieving, the formula (line 21)
reinforces the theme and further specifies where the speaker is.
Poem 188, in which the formula *wo hsing ch'i yeh* 我行其野 repeats
three times to usher in each stanza, is intensified by the pattern of
plant-plucking, the motif which is explained in the stanzas themselves as a gesture expressive of the desire to return. The feminine
voice is extraordinarily firm:

(2) 我行其野，言采其蓫。 *wo hsing ch'i yeh, yen ts'ai ch'i chu.*
　　昏姻之故，言就爾宿； *hun yin chih ku, yen chiu erh su;*
　　爾不我畜，言歸斯復。 *erh pu wo ch'u, yen kuei szu fu.*　　　9–10

(2) I walk into the fields;
　　I pluck the pokeweed.
　　It was as bride and wife,
　　That I came to live with you;　　　　　　　　　　　10
　　Now as you will not keep me,
　　I walk, back to where I came from.

And the situation defined by the initial formula and the plant-
plucking motif, as in the composition by theme, resembles the situation of poem 54: both poems describe the marital bond and the
fate of woman. In the formulaic composition, the type-scene com-
mands the selection of phrases, but not the individual mood. This
explains why the whole-verse formula (line 21) is apt for the
deserted woman of poem 188 as well as for the aristocratic lady of

[16]*Book of Songs,* p. 94.

poem 54, whose grief is related to the collapse of a royal house. The type, so to speak, is the woeful, helpless woman; and the scene is the fields where she goes to pluck some sort of vegetation.

CHART II: 101 (*Nan shan* 南山)

(1) 南山崔崔，雄狐綏綏；　*nan shan ts'ui ts'ui, hsiung hu sui sui;*
　　魯道有蕩，齊子由歸。　*lu tao yu tang, ch'i tzu yu kuei.*
　　既曰歸止，曷又懷止？　*chi yüeh kuei chih, ho yu huai chih?*　　5–6

(2) 葛屨五兩，冠綏雙止；　*ko lü wu liang, kuan jui shuang chih;*
　　魯道有蕩，齊子庸止。　*lu tao yu tang, ch'i tzu yung chih.*
　　既曰庸止，曷又從止？　*chi yüeh yung chih, ho yu ts'ung chih?*　11–12

(3) 藝麻如之何？衡從其畝；　*yi ma ju chih ho? heng tsung ch'i mu;*
　　取妻如之何？必告父母。　*ch'ü ch'i ju chih ho? pi kao fu mu.*
　　既曰告止，曷又鞠止？　*chi yüeh kao chih, ho yu chü chih?*　17–18

(4) 析薪如之何？匪斧不克；　*hsi hsin ju chih ho? fei fu pu k'o;*
　　取妻如之何？匪媒不得。　*ch'ü ch'i ju chih ho? fei mei pu te.*
　　既曰得止，曷又極止？　*chi yüeh te chih ho yu chi chih?*　23–24

(1) South Mount high soaring,
　　The sly male fox treads;
　　Broad is the road to Lu, open,
　　Thereby the daughter of Ch'i traveled to wed.
　　Yet once she made the way to wed,
　　How can you think of her anymore?

(2) Fibre shoes five by pairs
　　Ribbons on the cap are two, matched.
　　Broad is the road to Lu, open,
　　For the daughter of Ch'i to use.　　　　　　10
　　Yet once she took the road to use,
　　How can you be after her anymore?

(3) What does one do when he plants hemp?
　　Across and along he dresses the rows.
　　What does one do when he takes a wife?
　　He makes it known to her parents.
　　And once it was known to her parents,
　　How can you indulge in her anymore?

(4) What does one do when he splits firewood?
Without an axe he cannot succeed.   20
What does one do when he takes a wife?
Without a matchmaker he cannot get her.
But once he has succeeded and had her,
How can you touch her anymore?

Supporting Evidence

(1) Cf. 189/1; 202/5,6; 201/3; 261/3; 261/1; 300/5.
(2) 63/1,2,3.
(3) 105/1,2,3,4; 101/2.
(4) 104/1,2,3; Also cf. 6/1,2,3; 9/2,3; 12/1,2,3; 28/1,2,3; 156/4; 22/1,2,3.
(5) 101/2,3,4. Also cf. 220/3,4; 104/1,2,3; 169/2.
(4–5) Contracted formula *ch'i tzu kuei chih*, 齊子歸止: 104/1,2,3.
(6) 101/2,3,4.
(9) 105/1,2,3,4; 101/1.
(10) 104/1,2,3.
(11) 101/1,3,4.
(12) 101/1,3,4.
(13) 47/1; 197/1; 101/3,4; 145/1; 156/4.
(14) Cf. 210/1.
(15) 101/4; 158/1. Also cf. 41/1; 197/1; 101/3,4; 145/1; 156/4.
(17) 101/1,2,4.
(18) 101/1,2,4.
(19) 47/1; 197/1; 101/3,4; 145/1; 156/4.
(20) 158/1. Also cf. 37/3; 174/1; 255/7; 257/10.
(21) 101/3; 158/1. Also cf. 41/1; 197/1; 101/3,4; 145/1; 156/4.
(22) 158/1. Also cf. 37/3; 174/1; 255/7; 257/10.
(23) 101/1,2,3.
(24) 101/1,2,3. Also cf. 121/2.

This poem, like poem 54, is said to be related to an historical incident, and again the incident is elaborated in *Tso Chuan*. But the chronicle itself does not plainly connect the alleged story with this poem as it does the other story with poem 54. According to the historian's accounts, the incident behind poem 54 is tragic, about a princess torn apart between two royal houses; the story behind poem 101 is infamous, also about a princess between two houses.

But we have no further information as to the authorship of poem 101. The poem's lesser degree of historicity perhaps corresponds to its "folk" character; "folk" in the broadest sense. The structure, language, and mood of the poem indicate that it is not only of genuine folk temperament, but likely to have been orally composed. Also, by and large this poem is more typical metrically and culturally of the *Feng* songs than poem 54.

The orthodox preface to the poem initiates (or summarizes) the interpretation that it is a satirical piece which the nobles of Ch'i composed in censure of their lord, who committed incest with his sister, who was married to the Lord of Lu. The preface condemns Duke Hsiang of Ch'i (齊襄公), calling his act "beastly."[17] Commentators led by Cheng Hsüan have quoted from *Tso Chuan* to specify the incident which was the immediate motivation of this composition. In the first month of the eighteenth year of the reign of Duke Huan of Lu (魯桓公, 694 B.C.), the duke met Duke Hsiang of Ch'i at the place called Lo (濼), where the latter violated the former's wife, his own sister Wen-chiang (文姜).[18] The incestuous relations, Cheng adds, began even before Wen-chiang was wedded to the Lord of Lu. And in agreement with the document, poems 104 and 106 are usually taken as expressing contempt of this triangle, which disgraced the two houses and virtually led to the death of the Duke of Lu.[19] Including the renowned scholastic skeptic Ts'ui Shu, students of *Shih Ching* have generally confirmed the interpretation.[20]

In attempting to analyze the poem, we cannot afford to overlook the alleged historical background. Proper names scattered in the lines are mostly proof of the localities; it is the area between Ch'i and Lu that is celebrated in the poem. However, the ambiguity of "South Mount," which Ch'en Huan meticulously specifies as Niu-shan (牛山),[21] readily characterizes the poem as a substantially formulaic composition. First, we have no dependable evidence to

---

[17]Initiate or summarize: it depends who was responsible for the writing of the preface to each individual poem. For modern discussions related to the problem, see Ku Chieh-Kang, ed., *Ku-shih pien,* Vol. III, pp. 382–406.

[18]*Ch'un Ch'iu san chuan,* p. 93.

[19]*Ibid.* Karlgren is confused by the triangle relations and makes a grave mistake in his *Book of Odes,* p. 65.

[20]For Ts'ui Shu's confirmation, see *"Tu Feng ou-chih,"* in *T'sui Tung-pi yi-shu,* Vol. V, p. 23.

[21]*Shih Mao-shih-chuan shu,* VIII, 5a (p. 250).

prove that Niu-shan is "South Mount." Second, even granted that it is, the fact that the poet refers to it as "South Mount," shunning its proper name, indicates how in this type of poetic creation one would rather use a phrase of primarily formulaic character than make a more precise object-reference. The supporting evidence for the first line makes clear how *nan-shan* is apt to associate with adjectival reduplicatives (189/1; 202/5,6). Lack of specification in actual reference is one of the characteristics of oral poetry. In a way, it is also the lyrical singer's "thrift," which Lord reports to be scarce in the Yugoslav tradition.[22]

Another element in the poem which is significant as characteristic of oral-formulaic poetry lies in the seventh line. Ironically the line involves no whole-verse formula according to our definition. But it contains an essential formulaic element and contributes to exhibiting the formulaic nature of the poem by carrying with it an irrelevancy in the naming of objects—the five pairs of shoes which were dowries of the royal bride. The shoes are referred to as *ko lü*, shoes made of the coarse fibres of a plant which Karlgren glosses as *Dolichos* or *Pachyrhizus* and a contemporary Chinese botanist identifies as *Pueraria thunbergiana Benth.*[23] The word *lü* (shoes) occurs three times in *Shih Ching*, each time with *ko* as its qualifier (101/2; 197/1; 203/2). Among them, two of the identical compounds stand out with reduplicatives as the whole-verse formula *chiu chiu ko lü* 糾糾葛屨; and the third is in poem 101. Also, the individual lines with the first two occurrences of the *ko lü* image constitute an unmistakable cluster of formulas. The complete formation runs:

糾糾葛屨，可以履霜。 *chiu chiu ko lü, k'o yi li shuang.*

Fibre shoes tightly woven
Are good for walking upon the frost.

The whole-verse formula occurs identically in poems 107 and 203. Commenting on the latter, Waley notes that the cluster witnesses "at any rate a utilization of the same theme" as that uncovered in

---

[22]Cf. *Singer of Tales,* p. 53.

[23]For the former, see *Grammata Serica,* p. 206; for the latter, see Lu Wen-yü (陸文郁), *Shih ts'ao-mu chin shih* (詩草木今釋), p. 2. The plant is not entered in the traditionally authoritative manual, Lu Chi (陸璣), *Mao-shih ts'ao-mu-niao-shou-ch'ung-yü shu* (毛詩草木鳥獸蟲魚疏).

the former.[24] The cluster of formulas contains an irony: the shoes of fibres are coarse and thin and are not "good for walking upon the frost." In both poems where this specific cluster of formulas occurs, the poet aims at suggesting the hardship of a wayfarer in times between autumn and winter, when frost falls. For normally one wears leather shoes to brave the frosty earth.[25] Now, the *Spring and Autumn* (春秋) records that Duke Hsiang of Ch'i married his sister Wen-chiang to Duke Huan of Lu in the ninth month of the third year of the latter's reign (709 B.C.).[26] The ninth month when the bride travels falls in late autumn, as the seventh month mentioned in *Tso Chuan* is already definitely called "autumn" (which must be early autumn). And immediately following in the chronicle Duke Hsiang sends his younger brother to visit the newly wedded, a gesture of respect in accordance with matrimonial propriety—this happens in "winter." Then the year turns. The road to Lu is broad open, as the poem says. But we are sure that it is frost-covered, and the calendar poem (154) presents the line to support our assumption: *chiu yüeh su shuang* 九月肅霜 (in the ninth month is piercing frost).

Why, then, is a bride from one of the two most powerful royal families traveling in frosty late autumn provided with five pairs of coarse, thin shoes made of *Pueraria thunbergiana Benth?* No matter how well made for her in particular these pairs of shoes may be, five pairs of shoes made of fibres are absurd objects for an autumn bride to carry as dowry. Being the beloved daughter of a proud duchy that assumed the dominating position in China, Wen-chiang is well qualified for white leather shoes in the winter and fibre shoes in the summer times, according to the *Rites of Chou*.[27] Even if she is

[24]*Book of Songs*, p. 318. Waley is perceptive, but I wonder why instead of "formula" he calls it "theme." On other occasions (see pp. 321, 206, 117) Waley seems to have been exposed to the Parry theory of oral-formulaic composition.

[25]See Cheng Hsüan's annotation to poem 107, *Mao-shih Cheng chien, SPPY*, reprint (Taipei, 1967), V, 8a.

[26]桓三年: 春正月, 公會齊侯于嬴。夏, 齊侯衛侯胥命于蒲。六月, 公會杞侯于郕。秋七月壬辰, 朔, 日有食之, 既 . . . 九月, 齊侯送姜氏于讙, 公會齊侯于讙, 夫人姜氏至自齊。冬, 齊侯使其弟來聘。有年 . . . (*Ch'un Ch'iu san chuan*, 67–69).

[27]See *Chou Li*, *SSCCS*, VIII, 18a, and the Cheng annotation on 18b and the K'ung commentaries on 21a; also see *Yi Li* (儀禮), *SSCCS*, XXX, 1a. For the evidence that a daughter of a duchy may assume royal sartorial propriety, cf. poem 261, and Cheng's arguments in the *Chou Li*. Ch'en Huan

not wearing them and if the five pairs are merely ritualistic tokens of marital harmony, symbolic of "being matched," as many commentators are sensible to add, no document whatsoever tells that only fibre shoes make the ritual. Still it is more conceivable that the autumn bride has to be provided with leather shoes in pairs. This is lack of realism. Lack of realism is another characteristic of oral-formulaic poetry.[28]

Our rationalization for the ambiguous naming of the mountain in the first line, which is apparently constituted on the basis of a phrasal pattern, and our investigation of the unrealistic reference to objects in the seemingly unformulaic seventh line, lead to the conclusion that the poem is orally composed. A poet composing spontaneously (before an audience) makes use of traditional, vague, and sometimes "inaccurate" expressions as long as these expressions are capable of eliciting a fixed response from the audience when the paragraph, or the poem, is completed. "South Mount" is premeditatedly "high soaring," and shoes of any material in pairs are symbolic of marital harmony. For anything but the introduction of these notions, the oral poet is virtually not responsible; nor would the audience, one suspects, care. The overall degree of formulaicness as shown in the chart and the table of supporting evidence reveal a proportionate distribution of repeated phrases over the four well-balanced stanzas. In comparison with poem 54, the number of formulas particular to the poem, becoming incremental as they repeat, is much larger in poem 101. To an extent two-thirds of each stanza appears like an envoi; and the metrical pattern goes steadily. All these factors, on top of the fact that the poem is nearly

---

provides a comprehensive array of information proving that fibres are not the only materials of which the lady's shoes are made; see *shu*, p. 265.

[28]Lack of realism includes narrative inconsistencies, nominal inaccuracies, and the excessive, wild dimension of metaphor-simile reference. For the discovery of narrative inconsistencies as characteristic of oral poetry by Lord and Magoun, cf. note 18, Chapter One; for Homer's special mode of metaphorical analogy (the long simile and the uses of irrelevance), see Phillip Damon, *Modes of Analogy in Ancient and Medieval Verse*, pp. 261–271; for general observations concerning lack of realism in oral-formulaic poetry, cf. Frederic M. Combellack, "Milman Parry and Homeric Artistry,"p. 193n.; and William Whallon, "The Diction of *Beowulf*," p. 311. Also cf. Scholes and Kellogg, *The Nature of Narrative*, p. 20; C.S. Lewis, *Preface to Paradise Lost*, p. 20; and John Finlayson, "Formulaic Technique in *Morte Arthure*," p. 392.

100 percent formulaic, contribute to the conclusion that this is a
poem created spontaneously for singing, and probably after the
fashion of primitive communal singing. It is in this sense that the
poem is more typical than poem 54 of the *Feng* as a class of *Shih
Ching* poetry.[29]

CHART III: 168 (*Ch'u chü* 出車)

(1) 我出我車，于彼牧矣；   *wo ch'u wo chü, yü pi mu yi;*
　　自天子所，謂我來矣。   *tzu t'ien tzu suo, wei wo lai yi.*
　　召彼僕夫，謂之載矣；   *chao pi p'u fu, wei chih tsai yi;*
　　王事多難，維其棘矣。   *wang shih tuo nan, wei ch'i chi yi.*   7–8

(2) 我出我車，于彼郊矣；   *wo ch'u wo chü, yü pi chiao yi;*
　　設此旐矣，建彼旄矣；   *she tz'u chao yi, chien pi mao yi:*
　　彼旟旐斯，胡不旆旆。   *pi yü chao szu, hu pu p'ei p'ei.*
　　憂心悄悄，僕夫況瘁。   *yu hsin ch'iao ch'iao, p'u fu k'uang ts'ui.* 15–16

(3) 王命南仲，往城于方。   *wang ming nan chung, wang ch'eng yü fang.*
　　出車彭彭，旂旐央央。   *ch'u chü p'eng p'eng, ch'i chao yang yang.*
　　天子命我，城彼朔方。   *t'ien tzu ming wo, ch'eng pi shuo fang.*
　　赫赫南仲，玁狁于襄。   *ho ho nan chung, hsien yün yü hsiang.* 23–24

(4) 昔我往矣，黍稷方華；   *hsi wo wang yi, shu chi fang hua;*
　　今我來思，雨雪載塗。   *chin wo lai szu, yü hsüeh tsai t'u.*
　　王事多難，不遑啓居；   *wang shih tuo nan, pu huang ch'i chü;*
　　豈不懷歸？畏此簡書。   *ch'i pu huai kuei? wei tz'u chien shu.* 31–32

(5) 喓喓草蟲，趯趯阜螽。   *yao yao ts'ao ch'ung, t'i t'i fu chung.*
　　未見君子，憂心忡忡。   *wei chien chün tzu, yu hsin ch'ung ch'ung.*
　　既見君子，我心則降。   *chi chien chün tzu, wo hsin tse chiang.*
　　赫赫南仲，薄伐西戎。   *ho ho nan chung, po fa hsi jung.*   39–40

(6) 春日遲遲，卉木萋萋，   *ch'un jih ch'ih ch'ih, hui mu ch'i ch'i,*
　　倉庚喈喈，采蘩祁祁。   *ts'ang keng chieh chieh, ts'ai fan ch'i ch'i.*
　　執訊獲醜，薄言還歸；   *chih hsün huo ch'ou, po yen huan kuei;*
　　赫赫南仲，玁狁于夷。   *ho ho nan chung, hsien yün yü yi.*   47–48

[29]The best definition of *feng*, in my opinion, is still the one proposed by
Chu Hsi, *Shih chi-chuan*, I, 1a. Other arguments, old or new, tend to com-
plicate rather than explicate the term, which is to denote a body of compositions in substance, but is not sterile as an epigraphic fracture.

(1) I've had the wagon hauled out
    To stand on the pasture-ground.
    From where the Son of Heaven is
    Have come the orders that I be here.
    I've commandeered the groom,
    And told him to load it up.
    The king's business is to bring me many hardships;
    It is very tense affair, always urgent.

(2) I've had my wagon hauled out
    To stand beyond the walls.   10
    Here they set up the snake-turtle banners,
    There you raise the ox-tail pennons;
    The falcon standards and the snake-turtle banners
    Flutter flapping all around.
    Worry in my heart, I am very anxious,
    And the groom is already tired out.

(3) The king has ordered Nan-chung:
    Go and build my forts on the frontier at Fang!
    Wagons rumble out in array, many and powerful,
    Bright are the flags with twisted dragons and snakes in twin. 20
    "The Son of Heaven has given me an order,
    That I must build some forts on the Northern frontier!"
    Awesome, awesome is Nan-chung,
    Sent to have the Hsien-yün expelled.

(4) Long ago when I was taking leave,
    The wine-millet and cooking-millet were in flower.
    Now as I am returning,
    Fallen snow covers the road.
    The king's business brings us so many hardships.
    I had no time to rest, or to bide.
    Did I not long to go home?   30
    I feared the inscriptions on the tablets.

(5) Dolefully chirp the cicadas;
    Jump and skip the grasshoppers.
    "When I could not see my lord,
    My heart was sad, never at rest.

But now that I have seen my lord,
My heart is still, finally at ease."
Awesome, awesome is Nan-chung;
He has also stricken the Western barbarians!　　　　40

(6)　The spring days are long, drawing out,
Plants and trees exuberant in leaf;
Orioles sing tunefully in harmony,
And asters are being gathered, in abundance.
We have captured and tried the culprits,
And now I am on the way home.
Awesome, awesome is Nan-chung:
He has leveled down the Hsien-yün.

Supporting Evidence

(1)　168/2; 262/1.
(2)　Cf. 168/2; 15/1; 163/1; 178/1,2; 252/9; 278.
(3)　180/2.
(4)　Cf. 168/1.
(5)　Cf. 192/5.
(6)　Cf. 168/1.
(7)　168/4. Also cf. the thematically singular expressions in the formula *wang shih mi ku* 王事靡盬: 121/1,2,3; 162/1,2,3,4; 167/3; 169/1,2,3; 205/1; and *wang shih p'ang p'ang* 王事傍傍: 205/3.
(8)　Cf. 170/4,5,6; 214/2; 232/1,2; 233/1; 237/8; 264/6,7.
(9)　168/1; 262/1.
(10)　Cf. 168/1; 15/1; 163/1; 178/1,2; 252/9; 278.
(11–12)　Cf. 179/3 as a contracted version of the two lines.
(13–14)　Cf. 198/6; 199/1,3,4, for the larger formation based on the system *pi... ssu... hu... pu* 彼... 斯... 胡... 不
(15)　26/4. For others based on the system *yu hsin* 憂心 re-duplicatives, see 14/1; 168/5; 14/2; 40/1; 132/1; 167/2; 192/1,2,3,11,12; 257/4; 217/1,2.
(17–18)　Cf. 260/7; 262/3; 263/1.
(19)　297/1. Also cf. 73/1,2; 126/1; 127/3; 169/3; 178/4; 236/8; 297/2,3,4.
(20)　178/2; also cf. 283/1; 299/1; 177/4.
(21–22)　Cf. 260/7; 262/3; 263/1.

(23) 168/5,6. Also cf. 192/8; 236/1; 300/1.

(24) Cf. 168/6.

(23–24) Cluster of formulas: 168/6.

(25–28) Cluster of formulas: 167/6.

(25–32) Cluster of formulas: 207/3.

(25) 167/6; 207/2,3.

(26) Cf. 154/7; 300/1; 210/3; 211/1; 291.

(27) 167/6. Also cf. 114/1,2,3; 171/4; 186/1,3; 190/1,2,3.

(28) Cf. 41/1,2; 167/6; 210/2; 223/7,8.

(29) 168/1. Also cf. the thematically singular expressions represented in the *supporting evidence* for line 7.

(30) 167/1. Also cf. 162/2; 167/3; 197/4; 305/4.

(31) 162/1,2,5; 207/1,2,3. Also cf. 167/5; 200/4.

(32) Cf. 207/1,2,3.

(33–38) Cluster of formulas: 14/1.

(35) 10/1; 14/1,2,3; 126/1; 132/1,2,3; 217/1,2.

(35–36) Cluster of formulas: 14/1; 132/1,2,3; 217/1,2.

(36) 14/1. Also cf. *supporting evidence* for line 15.

(37) 10/2; 90/1,2,3; 116/1,2; 126/2,3; 173/1,2,3,4; 176/1,2,3,4; 217/1,2; 228/1,2,3. Also cf. 14/1,2,3.

(37–38) Cluster of formulas: 173/1; 176/4. Also cf. 173/4 for a contracted form of lines 36–37.

(38) 14/1,2,3; 54/1; 176/2,4. Also cf. 162/1; 167/6; 169/2; 26/2,3; 39/4; 146/2; 192/1; 196/1; 197/1; 147/2,3; 156/1; 173/1; 214/1; 218/4; 199/6; 225/2,3; 256/11.

(39) 168/3,6. Aslo see the *supporting evidence* for line 23.

(40) Cf. 177/3,5.

(41–44) Cluster of formulas: 154/2.

(41) 154/2.

(42) 169/2.

(43) Cf. 154/2 in the context only.

(44) 154/2. Also cf. 13/1–3.

(45) 178/4. Also cf. 263/4.

(44–46) Cluster fo formulas: 13/1–3.

(46) 13/3. Also cf. 226/1.

(47) 168/3,5. Also see the *supporting evidence* for line 23.

(48) Cf. 168/3.

(47–48) Cluster of formulas: 168/3.

Poem 168 (Chart III) is obviously one of the most highly formulaic poems in *Shih Ching*. The poem is relatively long and very
regular in metrics. It is one of the most discussed compositions in
Chinese poetry, singled out repeatedly by critics and scholars in
attempts to confirm their individual theories and assumptions in
relations to Chinese prosody. Of these critics and scholars some are
especially perceptive in using the poem to demonstrate the manifold
problem of *hsing*, notably Matsumoto Massaki (松本雅明) and
Shih-hsaing Chen in recent years.[30] Both scholars, like competent
commentators and lexicographers in the more distant past, see that
a few of the phrases in the poem are identically recurrent elsewhere
in the classical anthology. In the present study, this is the only poem
that I picked up not at random but for the purpose of reconsidering
the art of a formulaic poem through my proclaimed method and
of proving the serviceability of the critical method I employ.

The event celebrated in the poem has never been satisfactorily
dated or specified. The preface to poem 167 classifies poems 167,
168, and 169 as a triad about a campaign led by an illustrious Nan-
chung, a subject of King Wen, against the barbarians in the west
and the north, during the reign of King Chou of the Shang dynasty.
The triad would accordingly have been composed in the twelfth
or eleventh century B.C. Judging by linguistic and stylistic traits,
I have little faith in this opinion.[31] Two major historians of the
Han period attribute the campaign to either King Hsüan (827–
782 B.C.) or King Hsiang (651–619 B.C.), monarchs who lived
centuries later than King Wen, and these historians consequently
date the poems later.[32] For the following reasons I would associate
these poems with the reign of King Hsüan. First, stylistically the

---

[30]See Matsumoto Massaki (松本雅明), *Shikyō shohen no seiritsu ni kansuru
kenkyu* (詩經諸篇の成立じ關する研究), pp. 132–134, 297–298, 534–536,
540–541, 546–547, *et passim*; and Chen, "Generic Significance," pp. 400–
404.

[31]The poetic, linguistic style of the triad is too far removed from that
characterizing some authentic early Chou verses (e.g., the liturgic hymns)
and prose historical documents incorporated in *Shang Shu*. However, initiated by Cheng Hsüan, *Shih Ching* chronologists have always assigned the
poems to the age of King Wen; for the most recent chronology that absorbs
viewpoints of Cheng, Ou-yang Hsiu, and others, see Chang Shou-yung
(張壽鏞), *Shih-shih ch'u-kao* (詩史初稿).

[32]See Pan Ku, *Han shu*, p. 3744, for Hsüan; and Szu-ma Ch'ien, *Shih chi*,
p. 2882, for Hsiang.

triad resembles other important poems dated in that period, including a number of historical *T. Ya* psalms which invite fewer disputes than others as far as dating is concerned. Second, the commanding Nan-chung of poem 168 is also sung of in poem 263, which is self-evidently of that period. Third, King Hsüan, though glorified in practically all the poems attributed to his reign on account of military campaigns against the barbarian foes, is notorious to conscientious modern scholars for exhausting the people in the campaigns.[33] And the overtone of the triad is a mood of dissension appropriate in such a case.[34]

How, then, does the poet bring out the mood of dissension in a poem that at face value seems to depict the pomp of a triumphant army and extol its commander? In poem 168, the effect is achieved through juxtaposition of emotions, the "willingness" to fight for a cause upon the monarchal call and the hardships expected of such participation. The poem is prototypal of a significant class in Chinese poetry, namely the "trooper's complaint." It is prototypal of the complaint that does not become extravagantly emotional. In comparison, the other two poems of the triad are excessive in this respect, as they contain, instead of subtle revelation, bold statements of discontent.[35] Poem 168 surpasses the others by its subtle revelation of sentiments achieved through the art of juxtaposition. And in our terms poem 168 is a juxtaposition of original phrases about the present scene and formulaic expressions whose connotations are enriched because they recur in a good variety of relevant contexts.

Except for lines 1 and 9 which make an "opening formula" (within the poem only), the first two stanzas involve no other whole-verse formulas but are directed toward the revelation of sorrow,

---

[33]See, for example, Hsü Fu-kuan (徐復觀), *"Feng-chien cheng-chih she-hui te peng-k'uei chi tien-hsing chuan-chih cheng-chih te ch'eng-li"* (封建政治社會的崩潰及典型專治政治的成立), p. 47.

[34]Wai-lim Yip, in his defence of Pound's translation of poem 167, accepts without qualification that the poem is one of the triad of King Wen's period. Yip is, however, circumspect in concentrating on Pound's sensibility in choosing "sorrow" rather than "public spirit" as the proper emphasis in the latter's translation of the poem. The Pound-Yip opinion is of course not at fault. See Yip, *Ezra Pound's Cathay*, pp. 107–120.

[35]Yip, *ibid.*, p. 108, believes that poem 167, instead of poem 168, largely prepares "both the motifs and the viewpoint in all the subsequent 'complaint' poems of this kind."

in lines 7 and 15. The king's service is never easy in *Shih Ching* (see the supporting evidence for full reference). Closer observation reveals that in lines 7–8 the singer is stressing unwillingness rather than "public spirit" in doing his duty to the call to arms. The second whole-verse formula (line 15) makes clear the sadness in the singer's mind, and his worry. The expression *yu hsin ch'iao ch'iao* 憂心悄悄 does not necessarily denote a trooper's fear of combat. It is explained away by Chu Hsi who argues that the trooper's sorrow on a large-scale military occasion is only appropriate, because in ancient days a cultivated Chinese would be stricken by the same feeling at the outset of a great expedition as he would at a funeral: the feeling of sorrow.[36] Nevertheless, the formula is juxtaposed with considerable ambiguity with the reality that the groom is worn out (line 16). The combination, joined by another phrase of the same system (line 36) that personalizes the sorrow, reveals that the trooper is more bored than cheered by the pomp represented by the colorful standards and banners flapping around. Being an officer, he limits his feeling in an ambiguous formulaic expression so that he does not disgrace his breeding and integrity. Shifting the attention to a groom, the officer lets the stableboy translate his true feeling: tired, bored, unwilling.

It is behind this mask of loyal bravery and civilized patriotism that the poet proceeds into the third stanza. The guise breaks down, however, at the turn in the fourth stanza. In summary, the poem is divided into two major parts: the first three stanzas praise public spirit in symmetrical juxtaposition with the second three stanzas, which are an assertion of personal sentiments. Moreover, the poem is worked out on the basis of newly invented phrases of some systems in contrast with fixed (and probably time-honored) phrases that permit no doubt of connotations. The former phrasal type characterizes the first and the latter the second part of the poem.

The permeation of formulaic phrases on the whole-verse level and their tendency to cluster are the first stylistic elements that differentiate the second part of the peom from the first. Every stanza in the second part subsumes a significant cluster of the *Shih Ching* formulas. And with these patterned expressions, which are lyrical and personal, the poet ultimately gives up the mask he has worn

[36]Chu, *Shih chi-chuan*, IX, 18a.

for public performance. His unwillingness for military service is
uttered clearly in the fourth stanza, this time not through mention
of his groom's weariness but his own. But the expression of discontent is not yet extravagant, compared with poem 167 where the
similar cluster of formulas occur:

(6) 昔我往矣，楊柳依依； *hsi wo wang yi, yang liu yi yi,*
    今我來思，雨雪霏霏。 *chin wo lai szu, yü hsüeh fei fei.*
    行道遲遲，載渴載飢。 *hsing tao ch'ih ch'ih, tsai k'o tsai chi.*
    我心傷悲，莫知我哀。 *wo hsin shang pei, mo chih wo ai.*   47–48

(6) Long ago when I was taking leave,
    The willows were dangling in green;
    Now as I am returning,
    It is wet, the snowflakes flying.
    Dragging along the endless road,   45
    I am thirsty and hungry.
    My heart is painful and anguished,
    But no one knows how I have suffered.

In place of the lavish words that denote the pathetic (*k'o, chi, shang
pei, ai*) in poem 167, the poet of poem 168 makes sober statements,
maintaining minimally the dignity of his king's commissioned
officer. His sorrow is revealed in a rhetorical question (line 31)
and the answer to it, where "fear," the strongest explicit word of
emotion in the passage, is introduced. He does not appeal for
sympathy. And yet he succeeds in disclosing his unwillingness for
the service: it is out of fear not wish, that he has participated in the
campaign.

Whereas the fourth stanza depicts the grief of the soldier, the
fifth turns without signals to the solicitude of a wife. Again, the
verses are formulated according to some systems of the highest
level. Lines 33–38 constitute a perfect cluster of formulas, with
slight variation in relation to the first stanza of poem 14. And the
expression in lines 39–40 unmistakably belongs to another system,
which generates six modest clusters of formulaic verses in *Shih Ching*.
Three of the six occur in this poem. The susceptibility to recurrence
of the individual verses from line 35 to line 38 supports the assumption first made in Chapter Two that the *Shih Ching* language exhibits
extreme mobility, which is reflected in the fluidity of its formulas.

The meaning of the rhymed words *ch'ung ch'ung* 忡忡 varies, but the reciprocal defining power of the lines is conceivable:

既見君子，鯈革忡忡。 *chi chien chün tzu, t'iao ke ch'ung ch'ung.*

Now that I have seen my lord,
[Holding his] rein whose end dangles.

(173/4)

A variant of 忡忡 is 沖沖.[37] Karlgren's glossary approximates the former as "grieved" and the latter as "hang down." Waley, apparently influenced by contextual reading, translates the second line quoted above into "His rein-ends jingling."[38] In the convention of formulaic composition one formula gives rise to another; therefore, 忡忡 is so apparently a part of the *chi chien chün tzu* formulaic cluster that it can conjure up a sense of the equipage of the soldier returning home.

The last stanza also opens with a number of formulas which recur conjointly in another place (poem 154). The introduction of the spring days and aster-gathering motif would be difficult to appreciate if the specific mode of creation—formulaic composition—were not understood. Commenting on this passage, Ou-yang Hsiu says that it is delightful to put the enemy chieftains on trial in spring days when the plants are green and orioles singing. The commentary, appreciative as it is, is largely unwarranted. The details of spring, in my opinion, are a ramification of the "return motif" that is forever active behind the mention of aster-gathering. The lines that open the last stanza (41–44) flow from the stream of consciousness of return, both of the trooper and of the wife. With the enriched lines 33–38 in view, the spring days and aster-gathering passage does not seem abrupt—because it serves to reiterate the leitmotif of "return." This is one example of how in this type of poetic creation a passage (of formulaic verses) generates another without warning: one of the primary meanings of "composition by theme."[39]

The last two stanzas (where lines 33–38 and 41–44 combine to

[37]Chu Hsi, for example, takes the latter in his edition. Juan Yüan (阮元) gives a note in his collation of the thirteen classics; see *SSCCS*, X, 9a.

[38]Karlgren, *Grammata Serica*, p. 393; Waley, *Book of Songs*, p. 84.

[39]See Chapter Four.

give to the trooper's grievance a feminine tone of pathos) also surpass in artistic treatment the similar thematic import of poem 169, the third of the campaign triad. Many verses in poem 169 resemble these in poem 168. And yet unrestrained utterance like "the woman's heart is anguished" (*nü hsin pei chih*) is avoided in poem 168. Instead, through the utilization of familiar formulaic expressions, the poet has created this poem to embody many concerns which remain aesthetically allusive. To perfect a poem in this mode of creation, a poet depends more on his manipulation of phrases "with overtones from the dim past" than on seeking to formulate new phrases. Lord finds that some formulas lose their sharpness when repeatedly used,[40] but this only occurs when they are repeatedly used by mediocre singers. A qualified poet with sufficient imagination, like the creator of poem 168, increases the sharpness of formulas by using them repeatedly on given occasions.

In conclusion, although the poem's second half (stanzas 4–6) is comprised of more "stock phrases" than the first half (stanzas 1–3), the overall effect of the second half is no weaker than that of the first. What the poet ultimately intends is the presentation of the conflict between ethos and pathos, public spirit versus personal feeling. The presentation is achieved through the juxtaposition, in perfect symmetry, of the images pertinent to military pomp and the motifs suggestive of the desire to return. The juxtaposition shows the poet's full command of poetic language.

CHART IV: 204 (*Szu yüeh* 四月)

(1) 四月維夏，六月徂暑　　szu yüeh wei hsia, liu yüeh tsu shu;
先祖匪人？胡寧忍予？　　hsien tsu fei jen? hu ning jen yü?　　　3–4

(2) 秋日淒淒；百卉具腓，　　ch'iu jih ch'i ch'i; pai hui chü fei,
亂離瘼矣，爰其適歸？　　luan li mo yi, yüan ch'i shih kuei?　　　7–8

(3) 冬日烈烈，飄風發發；　　tung jih lieh lieh, p'iao feng fa fa;
民莫不穀，我獨何害？　　min mo pu ku, wo tu ho hai?　　　11–12

(4) 山有嘉卉：侯栗侯梅；　　shan yu chia hui: hou li hou mei;
廢爲殘賊，莫知其尤。　　fei wei ts'an tsei, mo chih ch'i yu.　　　15–16

(5) 相彼泉水：載淸載濁；　　hsiang pi ch'üan shui: tsai ch'ing tsai cho;
我日構禍，易云能穀？　　wo jih kou huo, ho yün neng ku?　　　19–20

[40]*Singer of Tales*, p. 65.

(6) 滔滔江漢，南國之紀；*t'ao t'ao chiang han, nan kuo chih chi;*
盡瘁以仕，寧莫我有？ *chin ts'ui yi shih, ning mo wo yu?* 23–24

(7) 匪鶉匪鳶，翰飛戾天；*fei ch'un fei yüan, han fei li t'ien;*
匪鱣匪鮪，潛逃于淵。*fei shan fei wei, ch'ien t'ao yü yüan.* 27–28

(8) 山有蕨薇，隰有杞桋；*shan yu chüeh wei, hsi yü ch'i yi;*
君子作歌，維以告哀。*chün tzu tso ko, wei yi kao ai.* 31–32

(1) The fourth month: it was summer already;
In the six month I drag 'in the heat.
My ancestors: were they not men?
How can they continue to see me suffer?

(2) The autumn days are chilly, cold:
All plants and grasses decay.
Tumults and wandering have made me very sick;
What shall I do, how can I go home?

(3) The winter days are fierce and bitter.
Whirlwinds: a gust blasts against another.   10
Nobody gets less than how much he desires—
Why do I alone have to undergo such troubles?

(4) On the mountains there are fine trees:
This is chestnut and that is plum;
And now, that is torn up and this is cut.
I wonder what crime they have represented.

(5) Look at the streamwater from a spring:
Now clear, now polluted!
Yet I have to meet calamities every single day.
How can I wait to become better off?   20

(6) Immense waters flow, the Chiang and the Han,
Main-threads of the Southern Land.
I have drained my vigor all to serve,
But why don't I have some support?

(7) Neither am I an eagle, a falcon,
That can flap and soar up to heaven;
Nor am I a sturgeon, a snout-fish,
That can plunge to hide in the deep.

(8) On the mountains there are brackens,
   In the swampgrounds, red thorns.
   I, a gentleman, have made the song,
   In the hope to release my sorrows.

30

Supporting Evidence

(4) 258/4. Also cf. 258/6.

(5) System of X 日 adjectival reduplicatives: cf. 154/2; 168/6; 204/3.

(9–12) Cluster of formulas: 202/5,6.

(9–10) 202/5; also cf. 202/6 for phonetic change.

(9) See the *supporting evidence* for line 5.

(10) 202/5. Also cf. 202/6.

(11) 197/1; 202/5,6.

(12) 202/5. Also cf. 31/1; 193/8; 197/1; 202/6.

(13) Cf. 38/3; 84/1,2; 115/1,2,3; 132/2,3; 204/8.

(14) Cf. 192/4; 255/3; 290. Also cf. 130/1,2.

(16) Cf. 40/1; 167/6; 194/2; 195/6.

(17) Cf. 165/2; 197/6. Also cf. 39/1.

(18) Cf. 39/3; 54/1; 163/2,3,4,5; 58/2; 128/3; 154/3; 162/3,4; 183/1; 167/2,6; 176/4; 183/2; 196/4; 220/4; 222/2; 245/1,7; 290; 299.

(19) Cf. 196/4.

(20) Cf. 33/3.

(24) Cf. 29/1,2; 257/1; 258/1.

(25–28) Cluster of formulas in contracted form: 239/3.

(25) 169/4; 218/1; 234/3; 250/1; 262/1, 3; 264/3.

(26) 196/1; 239/3.

(27) See the *supporting evidence* for line 25.

(28) Cf. 184/1,2; 239/3.

(29) See the *supporting evidence* for line 13.

(30) Cf. 38/3; 58/6; 84/1,2; 115/1,2,3; 126/2,3; 132/2,3; 148/1,2,3.

(29–30) Cluster of formulaic systems: 38/3; 84/1,2; 115/1,2,3; 126/2,3 (*pan yu . . . hsi yu* 阪有 . . . 隰有); 132/2,3.

(31–32) Cf. 252/10 (*wei yi sui ko* 維以遂歌).

(31) Cf. 198/4.

(32) Cf. 3/2,3; 252/10.

Poem 204 (Chart IV) is less formulaic than the poems analyzed above. The poem (a *ko*) is "made" (*tso*) by a cultured man who concludes it with a couplet of apologetics: he has composed in order to release his sorrows; the sorrows apparently come from his failure in public service. Whether he is an ousted courtier, as stated without warrant by many commentators, is not a question of high significance. "The identity of the speaker . . . is of little moment," says R. F. Leslie of *The Wanderer*, "but the depth of feeling he displays preserves his individuality in the midst of the generalizations, gnomic utterances, and formulaic patterns which give a wider validity to his own experiences."[41] In view of the many thematic and structural affinities between *The Wanderer* and poem 204, I have little hesitation in quoting from Leslie to begin a discussion of this poem.

The poet of poem 204 is evidently conscious of his individuality and of his personal status: he calls himself a gentleman (*chün tzu*) and appeals to his ancestors in the making of a "complaint." His concluding passage appears to be a formulaic variation of the finale of a poem which is demonstrably not a spontaneous composition, poem 252. In order to advance a critical treatment of literate, formulaic *Shih Ching* compositions in general, I propose to inspect poem 204 together with poem 252. The following chart presents the last two stanzas of poem 252 for analysis:

CHART V: 252 (*Chüan o* 卷阿)

(9) 鳳皇鳴矣，于彼高岡；*feng huang ming yi, yü pi kao kang;*
梧桐生矣，于彼朝陽。*wu t'ung sheng yi, yü pi chao yang.*
菶菶萋萋，雝雝喈喈。*p'eng p'eng ch'i ch'i, yung yung chien chieh.*   47–48

(10) 君子之車，既庶且多；*chün tzu chih chü, chi shu ch'ieh to;*
君子之馬，既閑且馳。*chün tzu chih ma, chi hsien ch'ieh ch'ih.*
矢詩不多，維以遂歌。*shih shih pu to, wei yi sui ko.*   53–54

(9) The phoenixes sing,
On the high ridge;
The dryandras grow,
At the place facing the rising sun.

41"*The Wanderer*: Theme and Structure," p. 139.

> Thick, green, the leafy trees;
> Melodious, tuneful, the birds in couple.

(10) The wagons of our lord   50
Are many in number;
The steeds of our lord
Are trained and fleet.
I offer a great many verses
All made for singing.

Supporting Evidence

(44) 3/3; 218/4.
(49) 167/4. Also cf. 252/10.
(50) Cf. 164/5; 177/5; 198/6; 212/1; 252/10; 260/4; 301.
(51) Cf. 252/10.
(52) See the *supporting evidence* for line 50.
(54) Cf. 3/2,3; 204/8.

The closing couplet of this poem reflects its maker's strong consciousness of social identity and his apprehension of the function
of poetry. This is one of a small number of the *Shih Ching* poems in
which an "ending" is designed with purposeful sophistication. For
the poems of *Shih Ching* are by and large worked out in a composite
convention, like that of the medieval European ballad, which requires
the perfection of imagistic coherence rather than structural acme.[42]
The author of poem 204, nevertheless, works more in the manner
typical of the few identifiable poets (e.g., of poems 191, 200, 259, 260)
than in the manner of the so-called folk tradition, where identification of the maker is not carefully incorporated. Like other poems
that include names of the makers or traits suggestive of literate
hands, poem 204 is only a little more formulaic than average, and
poem 252 is similarly terse. Its "coda" is a couplet virtually identical
to the closing couplet of poem 204.[43] Poem 204 (where *ko* occurs to
specify the genre) remains more formulaic, however, than those

[42]For a brief discussion of the composite convention as evident in poem
154, see Hua Chung-yen (华鍾彦), "*Ch'i yüeh shih chung te li-fa wen-t'i*"
(七月詩中的曆法問題), *Shih Ching yen-chiu lun-wen chi* (Peking, 1959), pp.
160–162.

[43]See Ezra Pound's argument about the structure of this poem in *The
Confucian Odes,* p. 170. Pound proposes to term the last stanza "coda."

which in the corpus seem literate compositions or those where the generic term *shih* is specified (such as poem 252). The author of poem 204, while literate, has very consciously chosen to call his composition the *ko* of a *chün-tzu*, i.e., man of high status, and at this point he departs from the phrasal convention of the poet who makes poem 252. In terms of the percentage of formulas, poem 204 is closer to poem 162 (where *tso ko* also occurs) than to poem 252, despite the fact that the singer patterns his last lines in the mode specific to remarkably literate works, including poems 252, 191, 200, 259, and 260. This, however, does not mean that we have much doubt that poem 204 also belongs to a "transitional period."[44]

During the transitional period a literate maker of poetry, not yet aware of any necessity for originality in phrasal attempts, would constantly make use of formulaic expressions from the vernacular of professional songmakers. Chia-fu, Chi-fu, and Cynewulf obviously belong to this class. So do the poets of the poems analyzed in charts IV and V. In poem 204, there is a conspicuous cluster of formulas, a contracted formation of another cluster of formulaic metaphors that recurs in a definite context, two groups of lines palpably of an important *Shih Ching* phrasal system, and other scattered whole-verse formulas and formulaic expressions.

But the factors resulting in the low percentage of whole-verse formulas in poem 204 are diverse. The first stanza, where verses of time-specification and verses expressing emotion are juxtaposed, displays a salient feature of the formulaic language of *Shih Ching*. Lines 1–2 are not formulaic at any level. And in *Shih Ching* qualifiers of the month (*yüeh*) occur in considerable variety and are hardly formulaic. Contrary to one's speculation, the more frequently a notion demands a variety of qualifiers, the less formulaic the notion appears in any context. There are over thirty individual verses in the whole corpus which denote specific months, normally followed by epithetic compounds of two words, and no two word-groups, be

---

[44]Concerning the dating of poem 252, opinions differ among modern scholars. Shih-hsiang Chen and Ch'ü Wan-li, obviously following the theory of Fu Szu-nien, attribute it to the period between 878 and 827 B.C.; Tse-tsung Chow contends that it was composed in the twelfth century B.C. See Chen, "In Search of the Beginnings of Chinese Literary Criticism"; Ch'ü Wan-li (屈萬里), *Shih Ching shih-yi* (詩經釋義), Vol. II, p. 232; Chow, "The Early History of the Chinese Word *Shih* (poetry)," pp. 154–155; and *Chow*, "*Chüan o k'ao*" (卷阿考), pp. 176–205.

they adjectival or other, appear to be the same. For example, the word-groups immediately following the mention of the sixth month are various:

六月莎鷄振羽	*liu yüeh so chi chen yü*	(154/5)
六月食鬱及薁	*liu yüeh shih yü chi yü*	(154/6)
六月棲棲	*liu yüeh ch'i ch'i*	(177/1)
六月徂暑	*liu yüeh tsu shu*	(204/1)

Line 2 in Chart IV shares nothing with others similarly positioned as specific designations of the month. In contrast with this, verses of emotional utterance are susceptible to formulaic patterns or systems. Line 4 illustrates this tendency, so do lines 12 and 24.[45] An explanation is that man's objective observation of nature, especially of seasonal changes, is more varied and specific, fresh and mutable, than his apprehension of human identity or even of his own feelings. This can also explain why the epithets for 雨雪 (rain and snow) are likewise variable in the anthology, with no two strictly formulaic. By the same token, the epic epithets for heroes in Homer and in the *Beowulf* are so extremely formulaic as to invite scholars to start with them in the investigation of the oral technique of epic composition.[46] And the Old English kennings vary more actively in naming objective natural phenomena, such as the aspects of the sea, or of objects produced by crafts, such as ships or spears, than in telling of one's state of mind.

If we regard the calendar formation variously recurrent in *Shih Ching* as stemming from a fixed system so represented: X *yüeh* A B, where X will be filled in by a numeral (which in Chinese usage

[45]Other utterances of "emotional" motivation, so to speak, include line 24 and line 16, the former formulaic and the latter doubtful. Line 24, however, is formulaic in relation to *ning pu wo ku/ pao/ chin* 寧不我顧/報/矜 (29/1/2; 257/1) and *ning mo wo t'ing* 寧莫我聽 (258/1) but not to *ning mo chih ch'eng* 寧莫之懲 (183/3; 192/5) which belongs to another system. Line 24 is doubtful because its systematic equivalent to *mo chih ch'i t'a* 莫知其他 (195/6) is only superficial, and their relation does not conform to our definition of the formula.

[46]For studies of epithets in Homer, see Parry, *L'Épithète traditionelle dans Homère*; in *Beowulf*, see A. C. Watts, *The Lyre and the Harp*, Appendix A (pp. 200–226), and William Whallon, "Formulas for Heroes in the *Iliad* and in *Beowulf*," p. 96 ff.

names the month in question) and A B by a coherent activity, typically as in poem 154, then we understand why there is not a single whole-verse formula to fit the relevant month (*yüeh*) exactly every time the month is referred to. The Greco-Roman tradition leads Spenser to treat each month with hundreds of dialogical lines in the *Shepheardes Calendar*. Chinese lyricism calls for rapid, precise statements of realistic activity to qualify each month, and the statements are made in virtually monological form. Considering both to be *lyric* poetry, we know that the proposed X *yüeh* A B system allows no identical words in the position of A B. For the succession of seasons is never only repetitious to the sensitive, lyrical mind.

One important formulaic system used in poem 204 concerns the naming of plants. It presents both unity and variety. Such a system usually serves as a type of metaphorical unit sometimes called *hsing* and sometimes *pi*. The system(s) can be represented as follows:

山有　X (x)......S–1

or

隰有　X (x)......S–2

or often a combination of both, which we may designate as S–3 for the sake of convenience. Following "mountain has" (S–1) or "swampground has" (S–2), X (x) is reserved for the naming of plant(s).

The system S–1 generates 10 lines in 5 poems, S–2 produces 11 in 7 poems; and the cluster of both systems (S–3) repeats 9 times in the corpus (in poems 38, 84, 115, 132, 204). In only one instance is the plant invoked to complete either of the systems repeated. Confucius takes the great variety of plants (and beasts) to be one of the advantages of studying *Shih Ching* (*Analects* XVII, 9).[47] The only

[47]The number of natural creatures in Anglo-Saxon poetry is slim. There are only ten animals in *Beowulf*, for example, according to Allan Metcalf, "The Natural Animals in *Beowulf*," pp. 378–389. In comparison, *Shih Ching* presents 99 different natural animals—the dragon is not counted—according to the illustrated manual: Oka Gempō (岡元鳳), *Mōshi himbutsu zokō* (毛詩品物圖考), IV, 1-VI, 6. There are more than 150 plants in *Shih Ching*. This figure is superior to those designating plants in other important cultural traditions such as the Egyptian (55), the Biblical (83), and the Homeric (60). See F. Kanngiesser, "Die Flora des Herodot," *Archiv für die Geschichte der Naturwissenschaften und der Technik*, III (1912), 81–102, quoted in Ho Ping-ti (何炳棣), *Huang-t'u yü Chung-kuo nung-yeh te ch'i-yüan* (黃土與中國農業的起源), p. 39.

plant that recurs in the same position of the system S–2 is chestnut
(*Castanea Bungeana Bl.*). The S–3 *shan yu ch'i, hsi yu li* 山有漆, 隰有栗
repeats in poems 115 and 126 (with a minor variation in the latter,
where *pan* 阪 substitutes for *shan*).

Now, the singer of poem 204 makes use of both the X *yüeh* A B
system and the equally protean S–1/S–2/S–3 system in his observation of natural scenes. Both patterns are far from fixed in the part the
alternatives (activities or plants) occupy; these systemic alternatives
are externals which one can visualize. They are in clearest contrast
with phrases denoting human feelings, either joyful (e.g., *wo hsin
hsieh hsi* 我心寫兮) or sad (e.g., *wo hsin yu shang* 我心憂傷). Phrases
of this class recur formulaically at whole-verse level. Consequently
there are a number of phrases identifiable as of a common systemic
origin, but there are not many phrases repeatedly used in the whole-
verse length. The *wo hsin* X X system yields whole-verse formulas;
but the X *yüeh* A B and the S–1/S–2/S–3 systems do not.[48] The poet
happens to choose two of the most sterile systems (sterile in the sense
that they do not produce whole-verse formulas) in composing this
poem. This fact is also a phenomenon of transition in the course of
the making of *Shih Ching*. The "course" is not necessarily the course
of time elapsing, but that of the enhancement of literacy among the
poets responsible in one way or another for the composition.[49]

At this point, my opposition to Dobson's view of the "stock
phrases" can be reiterated. Dobson thinks that formulaicness is the
evidence of "the individuality of . . . authorship," because, he
thinks, formulaic phrases are signs of "literary borrowing," some-
thing only an individual author would do. Dobson's conclusion is
hardly correct because the degree of formulaicness in the compositions of Chia-fu and Chi-fu (which have internal evidence of being
"individual") or in poems 204 and 252 is only modest. "Which if
any of the songs are literary compositions, written down when they
were first made?" Waley asks in an appendix to *The Book of Songs*.
Dobson, biased by his own presumption, answers that songs involv-

[48]See the diagram in Chapter Two for a demonstration of this assumption.
For the theory that a formula is remarkable only when it equals in length the
system that produces it, see Donald K. Fry, "Old English Formulas and
Systems," p. 204.

[49]Waley, who is careful in distinguishing a "poet" from a "singer" largely
on the basis of "literate" or not, notes that poem 204 is written. See *Book of
Songs*, pp. 304, 139.

ing considerable number of "stock phrases" are literary compositions, written down when they were first made.[50] This answer is
curiously opposite to the truth.

CHART VI: 301 (*Na* 那)

(1) 猗與那與，置我鞉鼓！ *yi yü na yü, chih wo t'ao ku!*
　　奏鼓簡簡，衎我烈祖。 *tsou ku chien chien, k'an wo lieh tsu.*
　　湯孫奏假，綏我思成。 *t'ang sun tsou chia, sui wo szu ch'eng.*
　　鞉鼓淵淵，嘒嘒管聲； *t'ao ku yüan yüan, hui hui kuan sheng;*
　　既和且平，依我磬聲； *chi ho ch'ieh p'ing, yi wo ch'ing sheng;* 9–10
　　於赫湯孫，穆穆厥聲， *yü ho t'ang sun, mu mu chüeh sheng,*
　　庸鼓有斁，萬舞有奕。 *yung ku yu yi, wan wu yu yi.*
　　我有嘉客，亦不夷懌。 *wo yu chia k'e, yi pu yi yi.*
　　自古在昔，先民有作。 *tzu ku tsai hsi, hsien min yu tso,*
　　溫恭朝夕，執事有恪。 *wen kung chao hsi, chih shih yu k'e.* 19–20
　　顧予烝嘗，湯孫之將。 *ku yü cheng ch'ang, t'ang sun chih chiang.*

(1) O magnificent and many:
　　The tambourines and drums we set up!
　　A thud and again a thud on them we make,
　　To delight our glorious ancestors.
　　It is for the descendant of T'ang that we play,
　　To assure that our ceremony is properly done.
　　The drum-beats reach far and deep;
　　Shrill, shrill is the music of the flutes:
　　Harmonious Ah yes concordant
　　Together with our sonorous chimes of jade.　　　10
　　O grand great is T'ang's descendant;
　　Lovely and fine the symphony of his!
　　The bells and the drums are splendid;
　　The *wan* dance goes on gracefully.
　　We have a number of welcome guests:
　　None of them is less delighted than we.
　　Long since very far in the past,
　　With ancient people did all this rightly begin:
　　Be meek and mindful by day and night,
　　Everything we do let it be according to the rule.　　20

[50]"The Origin and Development of Prosody in Early Chinese Poetry," p.
248n.

May they turn to us and enjoy the offerings
Which the descendant of T'ang has prepared!

Supporting Evidence

(1) Cf. 281.
(3) Cf. 178/3; 298/1,2.
(4) 220/2.
(6) 302; 282.
(7) 178/3. Also cf. 242/5; 298/1,2.
(7–8) Cf. 178/3.
(9) Cf. 164/5; 177/5; 198/6; 212/1; 252/10; 260/4.
(11) 286.
(12) Cf. 235/4; 299/4.
(11–12) Cf. 235/4.
(15) 161/1,2,3; 175/1,2,3.
(18) 254/3.
(19) Cf. 196/6; 256/9; 220/3.
(21) 302.
(22) 302. Also cf. 305/1.
(21–22) Cluster of formulas: 302.

The hymns of the Shang house collected in *Shih Ching* are only five (poems 301–305): the first two are obviously pertinent to royal sacrifices, and the rest are quasi-narrative of ancestral deeds. Poem 301 (Chart VI) resembles the other liturgic hymn (poem 302) and one of the quasi-narratives (poem 303) in metrics. Each is patterned in the form of 22 verses (with either 4 or 5 words in a verse) within a single, prolonged stanza. No other series of poems in the anthology is so structured, with such uniformity of tenor and tone, as to mark individual creation for a specific purpose.

Wang Kuo-wei and Fu Szu-nien, two of the most erudite and eloquent literary historians in modern China, agree that though the five poems are canonically entitled "Shang," they are hymns of the Duchy of Sung, enfeoffed by the Chou court upon the Shang descendents after the twelfth-century B.C. conquest.[51] Wang suggests

[51]The exact date of King Wu's conquest of the Shang empire remains under dispute. There are at least ten different assumptions: 1124, 1122, 1116, 1070, 1067, 1066, 1047, 1030, 1027, 1111 (all B.C.). The last, 1111 B.C., is most eloquently defended by modern archaeologist-historians. See esp.

that the hymns were shaped in the tenth century B.C.; Fu determines that they were composed in the seventh century B.C. and
reflect the brief, glorious policing of China by Duke Hsiang of Sung
(宋襄公) who ruled from 651 to 637 B.C.[52] In Fu's chronology,
then, the period of these hymns is approximately one century later
than the age of the *Ta ya,* which, he says, covers the ninth century and
the first quarter of the eighth century B.C.[53] Wang has given three
arguments in support of his own theory. First, Mount Ching (景山),
celebrated in poem 305 as the place from which the people obtain
timbers for building ancestral temples, is close to the Duchy of Sung
and distant from the area where the Shang people were once active;
there is no reason that the latter would have traveled that far for
timbers in the earlier phase of their history. Second, ritualistic terms
and technicalities of the sacrificial exercises performed in the Shang
house (which is said to rule China from the eighteenth century to
the twelfth century B.C.), as identified in the oracle bones, are
not prevalent in the group of *Shih Ching* hymns traditionally
called "Shang." And third, the phrasal patterns of these poems
resemble only those of the Chou poetry of the tenth century
B.C. and later: for example, poems 148, 178, 228, 258, 260, 262,
263.[54] Fu accepts the second and the third arguments but suspects
the validity of the first. However, he adds, the second and the third
are sufficient to prove that these poems are not products of the
period between the eighteenth century and the twelfth century B.C.
Thus, Wang and Fu establish a clear picture of the background of
this group of hymns: these hymns were composed in the Duchy
of Sung after the tenth century B.C., influenced not by the classical
liturgics of the Chou house but by the psalms of the *T. Ya* and the
H. Ya, in language as well as poetic vision.

Formulaic analysis leads us to a further consideration of Wang's
third point about the pattern of poetic language. The chart and the

Tung Tso-pin (董作賓), *"Wu-wang fa Chou nien-yüeh-jih chin k'ao"* (武王伐
紂年月日今考), pp. 869–904.
[52]Wang, *"Shuo Shang sung hsia"* (說商頌下), in *ch'üan-chi,* Vol. I, pp. 95–
100; Fu, *"Lu sung Shang sung shu"* (魯頌商頌述), in *chi,* pp. 58–67. For the
traditional dating different from that of the Mao school, see Wang Hsien-
ch'ien, *Shih san-chia-yi chi-shu,* XXVIII, 1–5b; and Szu-ma ch'ien, *Shih chi,*
p. 1633.
[53]*Ta ya* (大雅), *chi,* pp. 46–50.
[54]*"Shuo Shang sung hsia,"* *ch'üan-chi,* pp. 97–100.

supporting evidence reveal that poem 301, for instance, utilizes
formulaic systems in common with not only the Chou poems dated
after the tenth century. Line 1, where the exclamatory expression
ia...*nâr* 猗...那 is equated by Wang to *â* *nâr* 阿儺 (148/1,2,3)
and *â* *nân* 阿難 (228/1), is also related to poem 281, a liturgic
hymn of the house of Chou. Like poem 301, the Chou liturgic starts
with *ia* *zio* 猗與 ("O magnificent!"), and both poems are best
understood in a context of ritualistic exercises. Wang refers the verse
ia *zio* *nâr* *zio* 猗與那與 to poems 148 and 228, in order to locate
poem 301 at the time he calls "after the middle of the Western Chou
era," approximately the middle of the tenth century B.C. And
the poem also shares a similar pattern with poem 281, which is a
classic Chou *sung*. Shall we say, then, that poem 301 is contemporaneous with or roughly a hundred years later than the hymns of
Chou, which are generally supposed to have been initiated prior to
the turn of the twelfth century B.C.? If the answer is positive, we
are close to the assumption of Wang and far from that of Fu in
definitive dating. In general, however, we confirm their assumption
that the hymns were composed in the Duchy of Sung though they
bear the name of Shang.

For the sake of clarity, phrases analyzed in Chart VI as formulaic
and supported in one way or another by evidence from poems presumably composed before the turn of the eighth century B.C. are
introduced in the following list:

line 1: 281	line 9: 252; 260	lines 11–12: 235
(*Chou S.*)	(*T. Ya*)	(*T. Ya*)
line 6: 282	line 11: 286	line 18: 254
(*Chou S.*)	(*Chou S.*)	(*T. Ya*)
line 7:242	line 12: 235	line 19: 256
(*T. Ya*)	(*T. Ya*)	(*T. Ya*)

Line 18 even exhibits an association with poem 254 in terms of
preverbal Gestalt. The line is obviously generated by the word *yi*
懌 in line 16, as in poem 254 the line *hsien min yu hsin* 先民有信, of
the identical systemic origin, is heralded by the identical word *yi*
in the immediately previous stanza. If merely on the basis of some
phrases found in both poem 301 and the *T. Ya* category, one is
justified in dating the former in the period following the age of the
T. Ya, one may by the same token date the poem in the age of the

T. Ya, which allegedly follows the age of the *Chou sung*. For poem 301 also has affinities with the *Chou sung* category in the use of phrases.

I have made the foregoing arguments in order to suggest that it is not necessary for a *Shih Ching* student rigidly to assign a particular group of works to a particular period. It is not necessary to define the many "periods" in consecutive order by the rigid categorization of the various groups of poems according to the canon. This does not mean that one cannot make use of the poems to demonstrate a particular historical event, such as the catastrophe of Wei (poem 54), the infamous relation between the States of Ch'i and Lu (poem 101), the campaign of Nan-chung (poem 168), and so forth. Explication of a poem with recourse to historical circumstances is permissible, and narration of an historical event supported by information provided by a relevant poem is just. However, especially in the case of *Shih Ching*, an extant poem about a specific historical occasion is possibly composed at the time just following that occasion, but it is not necessarily perfected to survive (in the form in which it stands today) exactly at that time.[55] Every poem was over a period of time constantly modified and even drastically altered in language and structure. This period of time, "the formative age of *Shih Ching*," was an age when all the poems were undergoing the process of transmission. The period may extend from the dawn of the Chou empire through the age of Confucius. Until then, there was no poem in the anthology that could claim completeness. This explains why a number of verses mentioned in other classics are not found in the extant texts of *Shih Ching*.[56] Furthermore, this explains why the formulaic expressions of *Shih Ching* are prevalent in an overall fashion; the overlapping of identical phrases in various groups is due to the poet's limited awareness of different classes of poetic expression, and it cannot be regarded as the evidence of consecutive "influences." Except for the *Chou sung*, which I imagine a qualified poet at the time of their creation would fully understand as superior in status and function, the overlapping is ever present.

I presume a period which may be called the "formative age of

[55]Cf. Chow Tse-tsung (周策縱), *P'o fu hsin-ku* (破斧新詁). p. 37.

[56]For recent study of the problem, see P'i Shu-min (皮述民), *"Yi-shih k'ao-pien"* (逸詩考辨), pp. 117–163.

Shih Ching," during which few of the 305 poems were not mutable in one way or another. The texts were generally not fixed, and the style and phrasal features were fluid, sometimes because of the individual purposes of those who used them. But poem 301 is perhaps the best instance of a small number of distinctive poems composed by poets at the time when formulaic composition was still at its height. Each poem took its shape, probably as early as the tenth century B.C., and underwent constant modifications during "the formative age." The individuality of the composition of the whole group is manifest in the statistics revealing this group's paucity of whole-verse formulas (see Chapter Two). However, poem 301, as an example, embodies fragments of formulaic expressions from some of the rest of the classical anthology, formulaic expressions known to us as particular to categories both earlier and later than the specific group itself. Diverse features characterize the earliest-initiated *Chou sung* and the latest-initiated *Lu sung.* I would rather regard these stylistic traits of the Shang hymns as the achievement of individual composition, including the contribution from the scribe, than as a phenomenon of successive influences.[57]

The protean character of the basic meaning of a *Shih Ching* word also illuminates the individual compositional art in formulaic vogue when the tradition was ripe. Whereas in the majority of instances the recurrent expressions in poem 301 have the same meaning as when they occur in either "earlier" or "later" poems, e.g., *sui wo szu ch'eng* 綏我思成 (line 6) in relation to the same words in the *Chou sung,* and *mu mu* 穆穆 (line 12) in relation to the same words in the *Lu sung,* some word-groups attain meanings particular to this poem only. For example, *hui hui* 嘒嘒 in line 8, which qualifies the sound of the flute, is never similarly used in its other four occurrences: in those cases it qualifies either the starbeam or the chirp of insects. Also, the meaning of *yu yi* 有斁 in line 13 is unusual, with $yi < $*diăk qualifying the sound of music and therefore "*yu yi*". On all other occasions, the word *yi* means either "tired of" and "fed up with"[58]

---

[57]For the problems of linguistic and prosodic agreements among *Shih Ching* poetry of various dialectical areas, and the suggestion that the poems we read today are not the poems flourishing then, cf. Ch'ü Wan-li "*Lun Kuo feng fei min-chien ko-yao te pen-lai mien-mu.*"

[58]For the most convenient glossary, see Karlgren, *Grammata Serica,* p. 331.

(in poems 2, 240, 278, 297, 299), and therefore the compound is "*wu*" *yi* "無" 斁, or as an extension "harm," "hurt," and "corrupt" (in poem 258) and therefore *hao yi* 耗斁. For a positive connotation, the use of *yu yi* instead of *wu yi* is peculiar to poem 301, and the only reason seems to be that in line 13 *yu yi* may parallel *yu yi* 有奕 (*ziăk) in line 14. In a ritualistic hymn designed for one to dance to, twisting a word's meaning to suit some phonetic harmony is feasible. And the fluidity of these words may demonstrate the individuality of the poem at a transitional stage. The scribe, whoever he is, is perhaps "of little moment"; but the scribe has demonstrated his individual ingenuity, and his adaption of formulaic patterns has given "a wider validity to his own experiences."[59]

Poem 301, which apparently took its final shape, the shape in which it stands today, over a long period of time, is like a microcosm of the art of formulaic composition. Most of the traits of oral-formulaic poetry—its ritualistic,[60] pro-musical, para-dancing qualities[61]—as well as the array of phrases on the one hand evidently produced by prevalent systemic origins, and on the other hand in keeping with chronistic and regional colors, are found in the hymn. Despite the evidence that individual talents may have had their shares in the making of poem 301 as it appears in the modern text, the poem is representative of all *Shih Ching* lyrics in that its formulaic, traditional character, rather than its oral character, should concern us primarily.

[59]R. F. Leslie, "*The Wanderer*: Theme and Structure."

[60]See Lord, *Singer of Tales*, pp. 66–67 for the magical, ritualistic, or religious roots of the oral song.

[61]See Chen, "Generic Significance," for music and dancing in the making of the *Shih Ching* poem.

FOUR

The Theme

LYRICAL COMPOSITION BY THEMES

Noted critics of oral-formulaic composition since Milman Parry have recognized the important role the theme plays in the oral, spontaneous making of poetry. Serious attempts to define it, however, began with Albert B. Lord. But Lord's definition of the theme remains meaningful mainly, if not only, in the context of oral narrative poetry. According to him, a theme is "a recurrent element of narration or description in traditional oral poetry . . . not restricted, as is the formula, by metrical considerations"; nor is it limited to exact word-for-word repetition, he adds.[1] In general, Lord defines the theme as a "subject unit, a group of ideas, regularly employed by a singer, not merely in any given poem, but in the poetry as a whole."[2] Then, in a later, comprehensive treatment of the subject, he states that themes are the groups of ideas "regularly used in telling a tale in the formulaic style of traditional song." The groups of ideas, he allows, may permeate a collection of "songs from many singers from many parts of a country."[3] To Lord, furthermore, the theme is that group of ideas which, in the process of oral-formulaic composition, serves as a guideline to the plot, the larger structure, of the tale.[4] In the meantime, the formula, being the "group of words," builds the smaller structure, the line, in which the individual concatenate elements of the theme materi-

---

[1] "Composition by Theme in Homer and Southslavic Epos," p. 73.

[2] "Homer and Huso II: Narrative Inconsistencies in Homer and Oral Poetry," p. 440.

[3] *Singer of Tales*, p. 68.

[4] *Ibid.*, p. 69; "Homer and Huso II," p. 441. Also cf. Magoun, "The Theme of the Beasts of Battle in Anglo-Saxon Poetry," p. 82.

alize. Proposing a substitute terminology, Scholes and Kellogg observe that the "themes" are actually what Ernest Robert Curtius calls the *topoi*, which when constituted into an articulate sequence are called the *myth*. For Curtius also points out, "Originally . . . topoi are helps toward composing orations. They are, as Quintilian (V.10, 20) says, 'storehouses of trains of thought' ('*argumentorum sedes*')."[5] Within this frame of interpretation, the theme is primarily another mnemonic unit helping to free the oral singer from the labor of word-for-word memorization of tales.[6]

But besides specifying a "state of being or situation" to make it easier for the singer to continue a tale within the narrative structure under his control, a theme also contributes to defining the poetic associations and unifying the sequence of incidents.[7] The use of themes in oral narrative poetry is, therefore, to benefit the audience (or in our times, the reader), who may receive the manifold bearings of a given passage through reminiscence and mental juxtaposition of all the collective thematic implications that they know, without the singer having to express all his exact intents. The critical endeavor to explicate the aesthetics of composition by themes begins only when this dimension of the theme is perceived.[8] The thematic repetition is a unifying principle which shapes "the structure of traditional poetry into repetitions of traditional ideas and images" on a typological level, and each theme "foreshadows the context of its next appearance."[9] Robert P. Creed offers an articulate remark concerning the theme's significance in this specific mode of poetic creation:

> Every time a singer performs the same theme he and his audience hear and appreciate that performance against

[5]Scholes and Kellogg, *The Nature of Narrative*, p. 26; Ernst Robert Curtius, *European Literature and the Latin Middle Ages*, p. 70.

[6]Cf. Crown, "The Hero on the Beach —an Example of Composition by Theme in Anglo-Saxon Poetry," p. 363.

[7]Cf. Donald K. Fry, "The Heroine on the Beach in *Judith*," p. 181ff.

[8]Noteworthy works include Greenfield, "The Exile-Wanderer in Anglo-Saxon Poetry"; Bonjour, "Beowulf and the Beasts of Battle"; Crowne, "The Hero on the Beach"; Ramsey, "The Theme of Battle in Old English Poetry"; Fry, "Aesthetic Application of Oral-Formulaic Theory: *Judith* 199–216a"; and Paul Beekman Taylor, "Themes of Death in *Beowulf*," pp. 249–274.

[9]Taylor, *ibid.*, p. 270.

the music of all other performances of the theme. Whenever the singer pictures someone walking in a hall, let us say, he and his audience super-impose that picture on their trained recollections of every similar picture. Or, to vary the metaphor, the audience—singer included—hears each new performance of a theme *counterpointed* against all the old performances it has heard.[10]

Themes occur and recur in counterpoint in all performances and underlie each other repeatedly. Occasionally versions of a particular thematic notion can be totally disparate in terms of verbal structure. Two passages in the *Iliad* (IX, 658–661 and XXIV, 643–646) are regarded as strata of a theme—the making of a bed—although the "similarity" is detectable only in the sharing of a common formulaic system (a proper name + δ'ἑτάροισιν ἰδὲ δηῷῆσι κέλευσε).[11] On the other hand, some themes are put to use in a situation where they seem not required and may appear inconsistent with the narrative.[12] The *fugelas*, the "Beasts of Battle" in the Old English "Finnsburg" 5b, for example, *singað* untimely and at a wrong place. To modern minds, this seems violation of verisimilitude or decorum.[13] But it is allowed because what the singer expects in this mode of composition is to elicit from the audience a "conditioned response"—the audience's habitual awareness that the battle is to be as awful as other battles sung of on other occasions. The bird is symbolic in that its presence is reminiscent of all the horror of combats, but it may not be a fitting part of the description of the scene where the battle takes place.

To the extent that themes are concatenations of imagery, and Lord's earlier definition notwithstanding, not really integral parts of plot or action, they are not necessarily particular to long, narrative poetry.[14] The theme reflects a specific kind of poetic intuition of a given age, applicable to lyric *or* epic works. It serves in both cases to unify the singer and his audience by evocative memory of common "*argumentorum sedes.*" In formulaic composition by themes, a poet-singer has recourse to a well-established thematic

[10]"On the Possibility of Criticizing Old English Poetry," p. 101.

[11]Cf. Crowne, "The Hero on the Beach," p. 364.

[12]*Ibid.*, p. 371.

[13]Cf. Robert E. Diamond, "Theme as Ornament in Anglo-Saxon Poetry," p. 461.

[14]Cf. Donald K. Fry, "Themes and Type-Scenes in *Elene* 1–113," p. 45.

convention not exactly because that convention helps to prolong the poem he undertakes, but because the convention appears to his trained taste to comply with a situation in which the particular incident or emotion to be represented is located. A theme, consequently, is perceivable not merely on the condition that it is incorporated in a sequence of themes. Almost every individual theme is aesthetically explicable when compared and contrasted. Normally, we compare the occurrences of one theme in a definitive body of poetic works. These occurrences usually do not come from the same myth (in Curtius' sense) where the specific instance being studied takes place. Every occurrence of a theme may therefore be regarded as serving an independent function. It can be almost totally free from the progress of a plot. If it is relative, it is relative to itself—various versions of its proliferous self. None of the various versions needs take effect in the particular myth that any particular occurrence of the theme has once helped to define.

When Bonjour accepts Magoun's remark that the theme is "for the purpose of embellishment" and is not important to the narration, he almost opens the way to the defeat of the concept that the art of composition by theme is exclusive to the singer of "tales."[15] Most scholars of oral-formulaic composition, apparently preoccupied with Western narrative poetry, have stopped short of seeing that there are instances in world literature where a singer concentrating on the perfection of the "basic incidents and descriptions" of life and nature would perfect his songs, often short, by employing formulas and themes as pieces of a mosaic to complete a concatenation of imagery within a traditional scope and stereotyped principles of paragraphing. Indeed, what is variously called "theme," "type-scene," "motif" in this mode of traditional composition of the poem, is almost identifiable with the *hsing* element in the Chinese aesthetics of the lyric.[16]

A considerable number of the *Shih Ching* poems are composed with the aid of themes. The themes are perhaps limited in number,

[15]"*Beowulf* and the Beasts of Battle," p. 565.

[16]For the discussion of the various locutions of the theme, see Fry, "Themes and Type-Scenes in *Elene* 1–113," p. 35; and "Old English Oral-Formulaic Themes and Type-Scenes." Also see Lord, *Singer of Tales*, p. 199. For the equation of *hsing* and motif in the criticism of *Shih Ching*, see Chen, "The *Shih Ching*: Its Generic Significance in Chinese Literary History and Poetics," p. 377.

but their occurrences are many. Often a *Shih Ching* theme is heralded by some reference to natural objects which in various evocative
forms prepares for the fixed realization of the content. The reference
to natural objects intensifies the poem by association and reminiscence which the audience can be counted on to recognize. The
reference is sometimes explicit and sometimes implicit or even
cryptic. One of the most intricate aspects of Chinese lyricism is the
natural objects invoked in scattered places in the individual poems—
and some of these objects seem ultimately to be disconnected from
or analytically incoherent within the poems. Prominence has been
given to *hsing* in Chinese *Shih Ching* criticism; however, until
recently, *hsing* was treated as arcane or mysterious. One of the
approaches to the reconsideration of *hsing* at work in *Shih Ching*
poetry is to investigate how a number of the *Shih Ching* poems are
substantially structured in imagistic analogy with some stock
themes. Through this investigation I hope to make clear that, as a
world-wide phenomenon in ancient poetry, the theme appears not
only in the longer, narrative poems as mnemonic device, as some
scholars tend to think, but in both long and short poems as a uni-
versal means of formulaic composition that asks for spontaneous,
fixed response from the audience. Poems intended for singing, be
they narrative or lyrical, take the immediate approbation of the
audience as the primary criterion of success. And composition by
themes is the most convenient and appropriate method of eliciting
the approbation of the audience. As this is proved true in the
narrative tradition, it will also be proved true in the lyric.[17]

COMPOSITION BY THEMES AND *HSING*

The expression *hsi hsi ku feng* 習習谷風 (gently blows the valley
wind) is a *Shih Ching* formula. It occurs in two poems, opening

[17]The most important analyst of the formulaic lyrical poem so far, Robert C. Culley, who has discovered that a great number of phrases and
phrase-patterns in the biblical psalms are "formulas and formulaic systems,"
refrains from stating that thematic composition appears in the psalms.
However, he endorses the idea that composition by themes is possible in
"elegies and some kinds of ceremonial poetry," such as those which the
Chadwicks report in Russian oral literature. See Culley, *Oral Formulaic
Language in the Biblical Psalms*, pp. 17–19. Also suggested by Culley as references are H.M. and N.K. Chadwick, *Growth of Literature*, Vol. II, 286; and
N. K. Chadwick, *Russian Heroic Poetry* (Cambridge, 1932), pp. 210, 274,
284, 290.

individual laments. The total occurrences are four (35/1; 201/1,2,3).
In view of the established character of the metrical position which
it occupies and of its essential idea, we may call the expression an
"introductory formula" especially relevant to the lamentation in
Shih Ching poetry.[18] The critical tag that Mao chooses for such an
expression is: *hsing yeh* 興也 (this is *hsing*).[19] This is an example
of the essential *hsing* verse which is by its own right a lyrical formula.
Stanley B. Greenfield suggests that it is feasible for the student of
Anglo-Saxon poetry to investigate formulas by analyzing the poetic
expression of some themes rather than a given number of lines chosen
at random.[20] It is also appropriate to inspect the nature of *hsing*
by attending to the theme as a compositional device in the
Shih Ching tradition. Poems 35 and 201, where the formula *hsi hsi
ku feng* is utilized with agility as a *hsing* element to commence the
elegiac utterance, are a most convenient point of departure.

Poem 35 is a deserted woman's complaint. The first stanza embodies a statement of the general marital principle which a woman
believes in. The lines are already set in the form of direct address:

(1) 習習谷風，以陰以雨。 *hsi hsi ku feng, yi yin yi yü*
　　黽勉同心，不宜有怒： *min mien t'ung hsin, pu yi yu nu:*
　　采葑采菲，無以下體。 *ts'ai feng ts'ai fei, wu yi hsia t'i*
　　德音莫違，及爾同死。 *te yin mo wei, chi erh t'ung szu.*　　7–8

(1) Gently blows the valley wind:
　　Bring darkness, bring rain.
　　Try, let us try to be of one mind,
　　And have no anger in between.

[18]Aside from the Western studies of formulas which open a passage, e.g.,
Robert P. Creed, "The Andswarode-System in Old English Poetry," pp.
523–528, this aspect of the formulaic "writing" in the Japanese *Kojiki*
(古事紀) is discussed by Robert H. Brower and Earl Miner, who take a
stand against the "standard formula" that initiates an opening passage.
Brower and Miner think that the "pattern" tends to deprive the images of
their force. See *Japanese Court Poetry*, p. 67.

[19]All prominent *Shih Ching* commentators but Chu Hsi accept this classical critique. Chu calls the formulaic opening in 35/1 and 201/3 *pi* instead of
hsing: this change is typical of Chu's post-medieval attempt to "correct"
the Han scholarship of the classics. In turn, however, Chu is questioned by
Yao Chi-heng on the validity of the modification. See Chu, *Shih chi-chuan*,
II, 13a, and XII, 20b; and Yao, *Shih Ching t'ung-lun*, XI (p. 221).

[20]"The Formulaic Expression of the Theme of 'Exile' in Anglo-Saxon
Poetry," p. 200.

Pluck mustard, pluck cabbage: 5
Don't count on the roots' taste!
There is no flaw in my virtuous name;
I want to stay with you, till death.

The woman's verses are defensive, uttered in a succession of formulaic phrases (approximately 75 percent of the stanza), and
heralded by the seemingly hardly associable "valley wind" motif.
Not a word, so far, definitely tells of the fate of the woman, being
rejected, although the expression *pu yi* (line 4) betrays her absolute
compliance and submissiveness. This passage is followed by five more
stanzas of the identical structure (eight lines each) which enhance
the expression of her grievance by referring to the memories of the
good old days. Each stanza, furthermore, has some specific metaphors or similes which also indicate her slow movement away from
her husband's banqueting house. The substance of the poem may
be described as follows: A deserted wife's complaint takes the form
of a contrast manifesting how in the past she strove to help her
husband to go through many difficulties and was cherished, and
how at the present she is disowned by him because his house has
prospered and her beauty faded.

Poem 201, where this introductory formula *hsi hsi ku feng* also
occurs, has probably been misread by the majority of the Chinese
exegetic erudites since Cheng Hsüan. Until the twentieth century
not one important *Shih Ching* student broke the canonical line of
interpretation maintaining that the poem is a reproof against King
Yu of the Chou dynasty (周幽王), supposedly with special regard
to the deterioration of true friendship among men during his ma-
lignant reign (781–770 B.C.). The interpretation is questionable
because even in the age close to that of Cheng Hsüan the poem was
recited by Emperor Kuang-wu of the Latter Han (漢光武帝) to
warn himself against mistreating his queen, an incident narrated in
Hou Han shu.[21] Critics of this century including Wen I-to, Ch'en
Tzu-chan, and Ch'ü Wan-li have tried to separate the poem from
the allegory of politics.[22] For us, the poem is another wife's com-

[21]Fan Yeh, *Hou Han shu* (後漢書) (Peking, 1965), X-1 (p. 406).
[22]Wen I-to, *Ku-tien hsin-yi* (古典新義), in *ch'üan-chi*, Vol. II, p. 189;
Ch'en Tzu-chan (陳子展), *Ya sung hsüan-yi* (雅頌選譯), p. 177; Ch'ü Wan-
li, *Shih Ching shih-yi*, Vol. II, p. 170.

plaint composed formulaically by theme. Judging from internal aspects, it has nothing to do with the much reprobated reign of the last king of the Western Chou dynasty.

Poem 201 likewise opens with the formulaic phrase signifying the wind blowing gently from the valley. The phrase, moreover, is followed by a mention of the rain which the wind brings. The traditional rationalization of the "valley wind" motif (for poem 35) goes like this: when *yin* and *yang* are in harmony, the wind is generated from the valley. This, Cheng Hsüan infers, is to symbolize that marital happiness (that is, the establishment of a household of sons) depends upon the union of the husband and wife (coitus). Hence, in view of the fact that both poems 35 and 201 are the wife's complaints, the valley motif probably arose from an early metaphorization of the wife. This assumption is supported by a third complaint of a divorced wife in the classical anthology, poem 69. The poem is comprised of three incrementally repetitious stanzas based on the first:

(1) 中谷有蓷，暵其乾矣；*chung ku yu t'ui, han ch'i kan yi*;
有女仳離，嘅其嘆矣：*yu nü p'i li, k'ai ch'i t'an yi*:
嘅其嘆矣，遇人之艱難矣！*k'ai ch'i t'an yi, yü jen chih chien nan yi!*   5–6

(1) In the middle of the valley is the motherwort,
Withered and scorched;
A woman separated from her mate,
Sadly she sobs;
Sadly she sobs—   5
Suffers from her man's unkindness.

The metaphorical relation between the valley and the wife who conceives and reproduces is suggestively put forth later in the cosmogony of *Tao te ching* (道德經):

谷神不死，	The spirit of the valley never dies:
是謂玄牝。	This is called the mysterious female.
玄牝之門，	The gateway to the mysterious female
是謂天地根：	Is called the root of heaven and earth.

緜緜若存；	Dimly it continues as if to remain;
用之不勤。	And use will never drain it.

The general kinetics of a distressed wife's complaint becomes clear: it demands a definite motif, the valley. According to the traditional locution, the whole-verse presenting the valley motif is where the essence of *hsing* rests. The *hsing* verse, consequently, originates in the stock imagery which, in the present case, helps bring out the stereotyped sentiment of the deserted wife's elegy. The mention of the valley wind (or the valley in general) as the center of a *hsing* type of poetic creation in the composition of the wife's complaint is so conspicuous that the valley motif can be called "thematic" in terms of oral-formulaic composition.

In addition to the motif of the valley there is another significant element in the wife's complaint in *Shih Ching* poetry. That is the mention of plant-picking; it is found in poems 188, 229, and 54, where the frustrated feminine voice shifts quickly from direct wailing to relating plant-picking, no matter what social class the woman is supposed to be in. For instance, the cocklebur-picking on the hill is the scene which motivates the woman's grievance in poem 3. Three other tearful songs of the deserted wife, poems 35, 58, and 187, employ the picking of plants or a bird's pecking of fruit metaphorically in the development of the lyrical content. The plant-picking, being another important factor enveloped in the stanzaic structure of *hsing*, is therefore also of thematic importance in the composition of the wife's complaint, although it often goes beyond this category to serve in other types of elegiac songs.[23] This technique is peculiar to the *Shih Ching* tradition. The formative prototype in particular continues into the verse of the Han era. The "old poem" of the Han that deals with the subject of the deserted wife, "*Shang shan ts'ai mi wu*" 上山采蘼蕪, carries on this technical mode of thematic composition, and it also closes the tradition.[24] One of the reasons that the Han poem stands as the final lyrical composition using the convention may be inferred: the plant-picking motif has by this time lost its primary force for in-

[23]For a paradigm of the "plant-picking formula," see p.18.

[24]For a brief discussion of the poem in connection with *Shih Ching* 35, cf. Yü P'ing-po (俞平伯), "*Ch'i-chih liao-heng shih tu Shih cha-chi: Pei feng Ku feng*" (葺芷繚衡室讀詩札記：邶風谷風), in Ku Chieh-Kang, ed., *Ku-shih pien*, Vol. III, pp. 483–489.

tegrating a classical *hsing*. It has been transformed into an aesthetically stagnant expression designating an incident of a sequence
which fulfills the narration of a pathetic event. A theme in Chinese
poetry stays vital only when it is in some way intrinsically associated
with the perfection of the technique of *hsing*, for *hsing* is the key
to the ancient Chinese poetic art of *Shih Ching*. Now, the typical
complaint of the deserted (or frustrated) wife in the poetic tradition
of *Shih Ching* exemplified by the poems just cited can be described
as follows:

(1) reference to the valley (wind) as the essence of a *hsing*;
(2) recall my willingness to come to your house to bear you many
    sons;
(3) my suffering with you while you were in difficulties in contrast
    to my forlornness now when you are better off—i.e., you are
    tired of me;
(4) you send me back because you take delight in your new mate;
(5) I go into the field (or, climb over the rocky hill) to wail while
    pretending to be plucking some (edible or not edible) plants; and
(6) a general statement of the principles of marital harmony,
    sometimes followed by a warning, provided in metaphors or
    similes, for the unmarried girls.

In practically all the complaints, the thematic concomitants
mentioned above are present in one way or another.[25] The phrasal
patterns are often formulaic, though not always. In terms of imagistic development and the use of identifiable formulas, palpable
examples are the thematic as well as phrasal relations between
poems 188 and 187, between 187 and 58, and between 58 and 229.
In some of the typical complaints, one or another of the anatomized
elements stated above is omitted. However, every new element
brought in as substitute for an omitted element finds a parallel in
at least one poem of the group of complaints. In addition to the
concomitant elements represented above as integral to the wife's

[25]The aspects of the deserted wife's complaint are comparable with those
Stanley B. Greenfield summarizes for the "exile state" in Anglo-Saxon
poetry. Greenfield finds that an Old English theme of exile is formulaically
represented thus: (1) status; (2) deprivation; (3) state of mind; and (4)
movement in or into exile. See "Formulaic Experssion of the Theme of
'Exile' in Anglo-Saxon Poetry," 201n.

complaint, some other specific motifs also overlap among the complaints of the deserted wife. Such motifs can be tabulated.

TABLE 8:
SECONDARY MOTIFS IN A WIFE'S COMPLAINT

Poem	3	35	54	58	187	188	210	229
horse-riding	X		X					
river-crossing		X	X	X				
shoals of the river		X		X				X
banquet without speaker		X						
bird against fruit or grain					X	X		
leaves turn brown			X				X	X

In table 8 are listed the most significant motifs or metaphorical renderings of frustration which are not included in my summarization of the steps of composing by themes the "wife's complaint." But that these items recur in the poems of this group moves us to regret that prior to, or during, the time of Confucius, as Szu-ma Ch'ien claims, nine out of ten of the earliest Chinese lyrics ceased to circulate.

MORE EXEMPLARY THEMES AT WORK

In the traditional art of composition by themes, the singer's selection of specific images or motifs is sometimes crucial to the poetic meaning he intends, and sometimes hardly at all. The selection is important when an image or motif is particularly needed for inciting some familiar sentiment which only that image or motif can evoke—there are many instances of this phenomenon in the *Shih Ching* tradition. Partly because of the limited number of available references, perhaps, and partly because of his desire to invite immediate participation from the audience, a traditional singer normally tries not to depart from the fixed denotation which the image or motif has through generations acquired. A little alteration of the imagistic integration can sometimes cause great distortion in what the singer projects.

On the other hand, there are cases when all kinds of changes are allowed. In these cases, it is so urgent to fulfill a series of the thematic concomitants that individual recourse to casual "approximate patterns" is permitted. One of the salient examples in the European epic tradition of composition by themes is the "Hero on the Beach," which displays freer choice of the fabricated units. According to David K. Crowne, who discovered this epical theme in 1960, the concatenation of motifs of the "Hero on the Beach" theme runs: (1) a hero on the beach; (2) with his retainers; (3) in the presence of a flashing light; and (4) as a journey is completed (or begun). But Crowne also notes:

> The four basic motifs which make up this theme are often used quite allusively. In order to employ it as a mnemonic device the poet needs only to preserve the approximate pattern, and may refer to any given motif only by means of associations, or by naming qualities or attributes of objects similar to those of the things named in the "pure form" of the theme.[26]

That is how, Crowne observes, the battle-standard in "Exodus" 247–251 and the boar-image on helmets in *Beowulf* 1802a–1806 fulfill the "flashing light" motif (normally the sunshine), and the monsters in *Beowulf* 562–570a fulfill the "retainers" in the completion of theme.[27] Moreover, Renoir suggests that even the "beach" does not have to be taken literally. He finds in the *Nibelungenlied* that the "hero in the doorway" also meets the requirements of the first motif of the concatenation as Crowne summarizes it, because the hero is also "at the juncture between two worlds—that of the finite inside and that of the infinite outside."[28]

Of the two aspects outlined above, which we may call the "direct" and the "allusive" use of the theme, the second is perhaps more common than the first and therefore easier to understand. It is common in formulaic poetry, be it narrative or lyrical. The first aspect, the stricter observance of the concatenate thematic motif, seems to be more demonstrable in the short, lyrical poem than in the long narrative. A reason for this difference is presumably that the poet and the audience of the short, lyrical poem could better afford to concentrate on the detailed particulars of the construction

[26]"The Hero on the Beach," p. 368.
[27]*Ibid.*
[28]"Oral-Formulaic Theme Survival—A Possible Instance in the *Nibelungenlied*," p. 73.

of imagery than the poet of the long, narrative poem. In other words, whereas in the epic traditon the poet seeks the materialization of the myth while composing, in the lyric tradition he tries to improve the individual *topoi*. The higher the degree of concentrated attention one gives to the individual element of the poetic sequence, the richer and subtler each of the integrants of that element becomes. While epic poetry abounds in examples of freer and looser use of concatenate motifs, which are recognized in the Crowne-Renoir observation as allusive, exemplified by the occurrences of the "Hero on the Beach" theme, *Shih Ching* poetry abounds in examples of stricter observance of the thematic motifs. This may to a degree indicate the different qualities of the theme in the lyrical and the narrative formulaic traditions.

Boating: Sorrow and Joy

Five times in *Shih Ching* the material of which a boat is built is specified. Twice the boat is referred to as the cypress-boat (*po chou* 柏舟), in poems 26 and 45; twice as the poplar-boat (*yang chou* 楊舟), in poems 176 and 222; and once as pine-boat (*sung chou* 松舟), in poem 59.[29]

The poems in which the cypress-boat is mentioned (26 and 45) are from two canonically different groups of the *Feng* section, Pei (邶) and Yung (鄘), believed notwithstanding to stem from a common area, the state of Wei (衞). In both occurrences, the boat is incorporated in the introductory whole-verse formula *fan pi po chou* 汎彼柏舟 (floats the cypress-boat). Mao, in his comments on the two individual stanzas opened by this formula, remarks that the art of such composition is *hsing*. Poem 26, traditional and modern critics agree, is a protest of a woman with "secret grief" (隱憂) caused by "a host of small men" (群小) who attempt to marry her against her inclinations. She sails the river recounting her troubles, of which the greatest seems to be her brothers' rude refusal to help

[29]The English equivalents of the trees are in agreement with Karlgren's glossary, *Grammata Serica,* for convenience. Of the three, *yang* is the hardest to identify. Most students of *Shih Ching* have taken it, instead of the poplar, to be the willow. In a more general treatment of the plants in *Shih Ching*, I have ventured the distinction of the several species that are equally labeled as *yang*: "*Shih Ching Kuo feng te ts'ao-mu ho Shih te piao-hsien chi-ch'iao*" (詩經國風的草木和詩的表現技巧), *Hsien-tai wen-hsüeh,* XXXIII (1967), 124–143.

her out of the predicament. Similarly, poem 45 begins with the motif of sailing, and the boat is also built of cypress. Moreover, the grief of the woman is substantially identical with that of the one in poem 26: being caught in a situation where she is to marry someone against her wish. Similarly again, she cannot secure any family support in her resistance to the suiters: she exclaims that her mother is inconsiderate. The concatenate motifs of the theme are roughly as follows: (1) the cypress-boat; (2) unwanted marriage at hand; (3) no help in resistance from the next of kin; and (4) an unavailing appeal to the heaven–sun–moon statue, which is not yet personalized in the Chinese tradition.

From syntax and from the contexts we are certain that the moaning women in the verse do not have to go boating to make their protests. Nor do they have to be able to distinguish the wood of which the boat is made in order to produce the songs. In other words, boating itself is merely a stereotyped motif in a class of *Shih Ching* poetry. It has through these two poems become a technical ingredient in the lyrical art of forming the sequence of the narrative myth, but it is not a realistic description of individual experiences. The boating motif provides a scene with which the versemaker can work in this type of poetry, which consists in the brief revelation of sorrow or joy through the description of various moments of emotional discovery. This is also the quintessence of the compositional art that depends upon the aid of type-scenes. The origin of the type-scene in general (the boating) or of the image in particular (the cypress-boat) belongs to "the dim past." We can venture only an educated guess about it through etymological investigation and by referring to later interpretations of the key word, 柏, po< pɐk< *păk (cypress). The *po chou* (cypress-boat) constitutes one of the most distinctive *hsing* elements in *Shih Ching*, noted since Mao. The type-scene which the *po chou* evokes in these two poems is the situation of a woman under pressure who asserts her fortitude despite frustration. The word *po*, in its archaic pronounciation *păk, is phonologically identical with 迫, p'o <pɐk<*păk, meaning "to press" or "compel." The former is again and again used in ancient texts as a loan word for the latter, for example in the *Rites of Chou* and in *Shih chi*.[30] The English word "cypress" is not in any way

---

[30]*Chou Li*, SSCCS XX, 7a-b; Szu-ma Ch'ien, *Shih chi* (Peking, 1964), pp. 1413, 2584.

etymologically related to "press," but by pure accident it may well illustrate the Chinese effect of the *hsing*, the motif word "cypress" punning to evoke the type-scene, the woman "under pressure." The *sung* 松 (pine) in Chinese arboriculture is traditionally regarded as of the same nature as the *po*, "cypress." The *sung chou* (pine-boat) mentioned in poem 59 therefore has virtually the same import as the *po chou*; both specify the frustrated situation of a woman longing for home but unable to reach it. A slight variation, again by pure accident, is the corresponding to English: "pine" can be a pun with relation to "pining."

To approach the *po*, "cypress," from another angle we can observe later philological concepts, in *Liu-shu ching-yün* (六書精蘊):

柏，陰木也；木皆屬陽，而柏向陰，指西，蓋木之有貞德者。[31]

> Cypress (*po*) is a *yin* (feminine, dark) tree. All trees belong with the *yang* (masculine, light), but the cypress turns to the *yin*, pointing west. It is apparently a tree with the virtue of [feminine] fortitude, chastity.

Whether the assertion has other ancient bases or derives from traditional understanding of the *Shih Ching* poems themselves, I do not know. But this passage illustrates the point that motifs as *hsing* used for achieving type-scenes are rooted in a store of popular knowledge or belief and that such motifs as *hsing* are often used for broad associative purposes beyond the literal meaning embodied in the poem itself.

The motif of boating on the *yang chou* (popular-boat) expresses the opposite emotion, that of joy. The word 陽 yang < iang < *djang is phonologically identical, thus punning, with 揚 (meaning "uplifted"). Moreover, in popular religious belief, it is obvious that if the *po*, "cypress," is a *yin* tree, its opposite is the *yang* tree (陽, homophonous with 楊 and 揚). Although I do not think that the *yin-yang* concept at the time of *Shih Ching* was as clearly defined as it was later, the emotive contrasts in these two sets of poems are clear.

Like the cypress-boat, the poplar-boat only occurs twice in *Shih Ching*. Similarly again, the poplar-boat occurs in the only two occurrences of the whole-verse formula, *fan fan yang chou* 汎汎楊舟

[31]The quotation is cited from Murohashi Tetsuji (諸橋轍次), ed., *Dai kan-wa jiten* (大漢和辭典), (Tokyo, 1957), p. 257.

(floats and floats the poplar-boat). Furthermore, both occurrences of the whole-verse formula appear to be introductory and transitional, opening new stanzas which are respectively the finales of poem 176 and 222.[32] The introduction of both the finales in the two poems is abrupt, insofar as their overall imagistic development is concerned. However, the poet's sudden recourse to a common boating motif illustrates the particular theme at work. The sentiment to be qualified by the boating motif in poem 176 is expressed in one of the most unmistakable clusters of formulas in the *Shih Ching* tradition:

(4) 汎汎楊舟，載沉載浮； *fan fan yang chou, tsai ch'en tsai fu,*
   旣見君子，我心則休。 *chi chien chün tzu, wo hsin tse hsiu.*   11–12

(4) Floats and floats the poplar-boat:
   It plunges, it bobs.   10
   But now that I have seen my lord,
   My heart is still, finally at ease.

The density of formulas in this stanza is virtually 100 percent.[33] In terms of formulaic composition by themes, the motivated sentiment is not accidental but premeditated. It is joy. Joy is also the sentiment in the last stanza of poem 222, which is led by the boating motif. And the boats in service of the materialization of the joy in poems 176 and 222 are different from the boats in poems 26 and 45 which suggest sorrow: the former are poplar-boats; the latter, cypress-boats.

Boating is one of the major concatenate motifs of an important theme of the *Shih Ching* lyricism. As the theme may originate in ritualistic convention, the emotion which the reference to boating bears also develops, I presume, in accordance with the various materials (or ornamental patterns) of the vessel. The poetry of *Shih Ching* reveals that even in the otherwise identical thematic

[32]Mao does not note whether the stanzas are *hsing* in compositional technique. But judging from Mao's remarks for the stanzas initiated by the "floats the cypress-boat" formula in poems 26 and 45, I have no doubt that Chu Hsi is correct in adding that those two stanzas from 176 and 222 are *"hsing yeh!"*

[33]See the supporting evidence for lines 37–38 of poem 168 on p. 76 for the reference of lines 11–12. The systemic origin of line 10 is charted on p. 53.

composition, sorrow is formulaically introduced by the cypress-boat, and joy by the poplar-boat. The nuance of the phrasal integrant points to the explication of the sentiment. There is also a *Shih Ching* song of boating which tells of a "neutral sentiment": poem 44. As the sentiment is "neutral," the material of the boat is not identified.

Heteronymy of the Oriole

The subject of wedding in *Shih Ching* poetry is usually resplendent with familiar motifs. Among them the salient ones are the peach blossom (poems 2, 24) and the oriole. The oriole is an example of heteronymy in the thematic composition of ancient Chinese poetry. The oriole is named in different ways in different type-scenes to incite different, even opposite emotional responses. "Everything that happens or is seen on a wedding-day is ominous," Waley observes as he interprets poem 90, a prothalamion in which, instead of the oriole, the cock crows on a chilly, rainy day.[34] It is perhaps because of the belief in the ominousness of everything happening or seen on the wedding-day that the singer-poet of that ancient period was inclined to adorn his nuptial hymns with imagery that had through generations of celebrating the ceremony acquired some positive portentous power. Anything that even the bystander speaks of concerning the ceremony may have some sort of contagious effect to foreshadow weal or woe for the marriage. The guests of the wedding would know this as well as the qualified poet. When the poet composes a nuptial ode, he would be extremely careful in utilizing the familiar references at his disposal, in order to avoid a bad slip. For example, mentioning fish is good because it is symbolic of fertility.[35] Therefore, at a time when formulaic composition prevailed along with the notion of contagion, poetic references to visible objects which fit the particular occasion would logically be limited. In most cases the mentioned objects are not necessarily what the poet sees at the moment he composes but are drawn from the stock phrases at his professional disposal. This can be regarded as one of the reasons that formulaic composition is practiced by the singer of lyrical poetry on sensitive occasions.

[34] *Book of Songs*, p. 85.

[35] Cf. Wen I-to, "*Shuo yü*" (說魚), in *ch'üan-chi*, Vol. I, pp. 117–138. Also see Waley's prefaces to poems 24 and 104 in *Book of Songs*, pp. 78–79.

The mention of the oriole in the nuptial hymn means a test of the poet's prudence in his manipulation of the heteronymy. There are several equally acceptable appellations for the bird called "oriole" in English, and the poet must choose the one that suits his verse the best. In the *Shih Ching* tradition, *ts'ang-keng* 倉庚 and *huang-niao* 黃鳥 are individually recurrent appellations for the oriole.[36] Reference to uses of both appellations shows that in this convention of composition, the choice of either affects the ultimate signification of the poem. *Ts'ang-keng* appears to be the appellative motif for the intensification of cheerful, blissful moments such as the wedding ceremony; for example, in poems 154, 156, and 168. *Huang-niao* is for motivating mournful, wailing songs such as poems 32, 131, 187, and 230.

In poem 154, the *ts'ang-keng* motif appears in concert with the important cluster of formulas about the woman's aster-gathering, which throughout the classical anthology constitutes the leitmotif of return (*kuei* 歸), sometimes signifying a girl's union in marriage.[37] Like the oriole singing in the last stanza of poem 168, where this leitmotif is also predominant, the *ts'ang-keng* in poem 154 celebrates the theme of the wedding.

(2) 春日載陽，有鳴倉庚：　　*ch'un jih tsai yang, yu ming ts'ang keng:*
女執懿筐，遵彼微行，　　　*nü chih yi k'uang, tsun pi wei hang,*
　　爰求柔桑。　　　　　　　　　*yüan ch'iu jou sang.*
春日遲遲，采蘩祁祁，　　　　*ch'un jih ch'ih ch'ih, ts'ai fan ch'i ch'i,*
女心傷悲，殆及公子　　　　　*nü hsin shang pei, tai chi kung tzu*
同歸。　　　　　　　　　　　　*t'ung kuei.*　　　　　　19–20

(2) In the spring days it grows warm,
　　And the orioles are singing:
　　The girl takes her deep, pretty basket,
　　And follows the small paths　　　　　　　　　15
　　To seek the soft mulberry-leaves.
　　The spring days are long, drawing out,
　　And asters are being gathered, in abundance.
　　The girl's heart is sick and sad,
　　Likely, she is going to return with her lord.　　　20

[36]For the different names of the oriole in the Chinese landscape and letters, see Lu Chi, *Mao-shih ts'ao-mu-niao-shou-ch'ung-yü shu*, p. 44.
[37]Cf. poems 13 and 168.

This passage, though concluding with the mention of a girl's fear in view of a marriage, suggests bliss rather than woe. This appreciation of the poem is based particularly upon the oriole motif unerringly defined as the *ts'ang-keng* and also upon the separate judgment that the theme expresses the complex psychological problems of a persona, the aster-picking girl. Her heart is "sick and sad," but she is by no means wailing or mournful. A girl on the eve of her wedding day, it is imaginable, cannot help having fear which may lead her to the sadness in heart revealed in line 19. This sadness in heart, however, does not darken but makes cheerful an "occasion," one which the nuptials by definition qualify as blissful. The orioles as *ts'ang-keng* flutter in the previous lines to underlie the atmosphere of joy which the passage overall is meant to convey, not the momentary fear or sadness of the girl herself. Her personal sentiments are diluted and finally replaced by the community sentiments expressed by the imagistic equivalents of the flight of the *ts'ang-keng* when the spring days are "long drawing out."

The *ts'ang-keng* in poem 156 appears even more obviously to be part of a lyrical theme of long standing, derived from remote, primitive customs turned stereotyped in poetry. Waley calls poem 156 "a typical 'elliptical ballad,' in which themes are juxtaposed." This view, unprecedented as it is, justifies his interpretation that the homeward soldier is musing that perhaps since he went to the war, his wife, assuming his death, has married again. The *ts'ang-keng* motif follows the introductory formula which in every stanza states that it is drizzling now as the soldier is returning home from the battle. Then unexpectedly in the last stanza the singer-soldier turns to the oriole in flight, whose wings are "glistening" (*yi yao* 熠燿). The adjective *yi yao*, "glistening," also occurs in the second stanza of the poem to qualify the light of the glowworm. In the last stanza, *yi yao* changes to describe a vision of joy. The effect is achieved through the use of the theme that admits the *ts'ang-keng* as a primary integral motif. The fact may indicate that in the oral poet's practice, the completion of a wedding theme by successively bringing in all the contributory elements is more urgent than imagistic or logical congruity. The wistful mood of the song obviously calls for the *huang-niao*; the singer, nevertheless, is so preoccupied by the convention of thematic composition that he utters *ts'ang-keng* as the appellation of the oriole, as if to effect the familiar, cheerful atmosphere of a wedding scene. The fact that poem 156 does not make use of the *huang-niao,* which suggests woe, indicates how in this mode of poetic creation a singer is controlled by the swift ebb and flow of the concatenate motifs of a theme. None of the prothalamia or epithalamia in the *Shih Ching* tradition employs this appellation of the oriole, *huang-niao,* and this is why our singer does not use it either: it was a time when poetry was "traditional" in imagery as well as language.

Huang-niao occurs in five poems, of which four are definitely sorrowful utterances. The devout poet of poem 32 regrets in ironical tone how he and his brothers seem to have afflicted their mother's heart, and the sorrowful thought is set off by reference to the "bright-looking, lovely" oriole *huang-niao.* Likewise, *huang-niao* is essential of the *hsing* in all three stanzas of a dirge (131) for three illustrious retainers of Duke Mu of Ch'in (秦穆公). Upon the death of the Duke, 621 B.C., Yen-hsi, Chung-hang, and Ch'ien-hu, all of the clan of Tzu-chü, were honored by the royal order to follow him into the grave. The chirps of the oriole never cease, occurring throughout the poem, as the three leading warriors of the state fall in the dirge sung by their admirers. Poem 230, another trooper's complaint about the hardships of military campaign, presents three times the formula containing the particular appellation of the oriole as *hsing: mien man huang niao* 緜蠻黃鳥 (pretty, little yellow birds). The fourth poem of pathetic outbursts echoed by the motif of the *huang-niao* is a deserted wife's wailing (187). Here the use of *huang-niao* as the appellation of the bird (instead of *ts'ang-keng*) is especially interesting in view of the persona's situation. The woman, rejected by her husband, is being sent back to her kin. On her wedding day the oriole may have been invoked as *ts'ang-keng* by a singer to finish a nuptial song that blesses her, then a bride, and her groom; on the day of rejection she sings of her own emotions, and the invoked oriole is designated as *huang-niao* to underlie the wailing sentiment. Poem 2 also exhibits a refined distinction between the motifs of *huang-niao* and *ts'ang-keng,* heteronyms of the oriole used in opposite human situations. Poem 2 is not a lament; but the woman (still a bride, apparently) pronounces in monologue in the last verse that she is busy preparing to visit her parents (歸寧父母), that is, to go away from her husband. In no place does she express any dissatisfaction with her husband, and therefore it is not a wife's complaint by my definition, although the *huang-niao* motif is incorporated in the classic *hsing* stanza. The poem shows how firmly the *huang-niao* and the *ts'ang-keng* motifs are individually established in thematic creation as regards marital relationship. For a new bride to visit her parents, away from her husband's home temporarily, there may even be joy, though of a different kind, rather than sorrow. But *ts'ang-keng* may have been too strongly associated with the union of mates. The trip, though hardly sorrowful, does not match a nuptial occasion, as it involves some ambiguity. But if the mention of *huang-niao* should conjure up anything doleful, a mixture of joy is effected by the poem's resorting to a formulaic expression which usually evokes freedom and bliss. The phrase *huang niao yü fei* 黃鳥于飛 (the oriole in flight) is patterned according to the formulaic system, "X X *yü fei*" (28/1,2,3; 33/1,2; 156/4; 181/1,2,3; 216/1; 252/7,8; 278; 298). In addition, the woman makes use of other formulaic expressions customarily associated with the auspicious *ts'ang-keng*, such as *chieh chieh* 嗜嗜 (see lines 42–43 of poem 168). The bird must be called *huang-niao* because that appellation satisfies the formulaic convention governing the usage of the heteronymous oriole motif.

The Bird of the Filial Return

The bird is an important figure in literature, especially in early literature; in many places, symbolic function seems to be archetypical, active in literature East and West. Concerning the bird motif revealing itself in the flexibility of the thematic concatenation in formulaic composition, such as allowed of the treatment of the "Hero on the Beach," the Chinese counterpart is the "Bird of the Filial Return."[38]

The "Bird of the Filial Return" differs from the oriole related above in that the oriole in different appellations provides specific nuances of poetic signification, whereas the bird of the filial return is a collective motif regardless of its species. The former demonstrates the assumption made at the outset of the chapter that the nominal specification of some imagistic references is essential in composition by themes. The latter proves the other assumption: in composition by themes the fulfillment of a sequence of concate-

[38]Cf. notes 27 and 28, Chapter Four.

nate motifs is so urgent that the poet, confronted with the necessity of bringing in a bird-image, may make use of a bird of any genus. Table 9 shows that there are nine poems in *Shih Ching* in which thinking of one's parents—or filial piety in general—is prepared for or reiterated by the mention of a bird.[39]

TABLE 9

THE BIRD OF THE FILIAL RETURN

Poem	The Bird	Function
2	oriole (*huang-niao*)	*hsing* (M)
32	oriole (*huag-niao*)	*hsing* (C)
121	bustard	*hsing* (M)
162	turtledove	*hsing* (C)
183	kite	*hsing* (C)
187	oriole (*huang-niao*)	*hsing* (M)
192	crow	*fu* (C)
196	turtledove	*hsing* (M)
	wagtail	*hsing* (C)
	haw-finch	*hsing* (C)
197	crow	*hsing* (M)
	pheasant	*hsing* (C)

In comparison with the number of poems in the whole corpus containing the thematic relation between the bird and filial piety, the poems where the bird signifies "return" but without specific reference to filial sentiments are rare: only poems 181 and 230 belong to this class. And poems that express the wayfarer's filial sentiments in his desire to return to his parents but without recourse to the bird motif are three (poems 110, 169, and 205).[40] The "Bird of the Filial Return" appears to be a prominent theme in the formulaic composition of the *Shih Ching* tradition.

The birds in the concatenation of the "filial return" vary in

[39]This indicates the compositional function of the bird in the traditional *fu-pi-hsing* poetics. In order to test the established findings of the past authorities, I have chosen not to interpret but simply take down the remark of Mao. In the cases when Mao fails to provide one, I take down that given by Chu.

[40]Poem 205 is apparently in close relation with the prototypal filial-soldier songs of desire to return, poems 121 and 162; the omission of the bird motif appears to be accidental.

species.* There are three appearances of the oriole, and it is referred to as *huang-niao,* to free it from marital or sexual associations. Two of the three are definitely songs of the wedded woman returning to her parental home.[41] A third (poem 32), however, seems to be a general comment on filial piety which any species of bird can evoke:

(4) 睍睆黃鳥，載其好音； *hsien huan huang niao, tsai ch'i hao yin;*
　　有子七人，莫慰母心。 *yu tzu ch'i jen, mo wei mu hsin.* 　　15–16

(4) Bright, good-looking is the yellow bird,
　　And beautiful its tune;
　　There are sons to her, seven, 　　　　　　　　　　　　15
　　But none could comfort the mother's heart.

The context of the poem suggests an avian behavior, common to most birds, which the Chinese believe has general attributes appropriate to allusions of human filial piety: the bird "returns to feed" (返哺) its parents. The yellow bird (oriole) is presented here to contrast with the seven sons who fail to comfort their mother's heart. The passage, therefore, may be regarded as exemplifying the basic notion that generates the theme of the "Bird of the Filial Return." While I do not think that all the poems involving the theme derive from these lines, I am suggesting a possible reason why all birds, regardless of species with few exceptions, could be used by ancient Chinese poets as motifs to introduce filial piety. The bird of the filial return, consequently, does not have to be any particular bird, not necessarily the oriole in poem 32, for example, for it is not the only species that feeds. Table 9 shows that in the nine poems of filial return nine different birds complete the theme. In poem 183, for example, mention of the kite precedes the wanderer's thoughts of his parents. This illustrates the ultimate freedom in the poet's creative, improvising process. Wherever the mention of a bird is required, he produces it by free association; even though the kite is invoked in poem 178 to be a "Beast of Battle," as in Magoun's definition, the poet makes use of it. The bird of the

[41]Nuptial songs celebrate the woman's marriage into a new house, away from her parents, to make prosperous a family of her own, and the oriole is *ts'ang-keng.* In case, for whatever reason, she returns as a child of her parents, the oriole is *huang-niao* which is active in the theme of the "Filial Return."

filial return, therefore, is representative of the type of concatenate motif in a theme that allows great variety in all details.

Table 9 also shows that of the twelve occurrences of the bird in the nine poems, every bird of the filial return but one (192) forms the substance of *hsing* which is supposed in traditional *Shih Ching* poetics to be the compositional technique of the respective stanza.[42] This fact confirms the assumption made earlier that the essential element of the lyrical composition by theme is almost always in correspondence with that of the composition by *hsing*. The invocation of the bird in the making of a poem about "filial return," in other words, alters a passage of straightforward emotional utterance into a *hsing*. If the motif of the bird seems only casually justified in the otherwise straightforward emotional utterance, then it is because the motif has in the particular poetic tradition attained some internal force and can prepare the poem for the experienced audience; this force we could not realize without carefully comparing all the occurrences of the particular motif. Concerning a similar problem, Creed thinks that close comparison is a modern critic's "substitute for intense and immediate responding to a living tradition."[43] Without reference to the same images or similar phrase patterns in different poems, the aesthetic implication of the signifying motif cannot be fully uncovered; nor, in Chinese terms, can the value of the motif's recurrence as the substance of a *hsing* composition be well understood. The reciprocal interpretative force of the motif occurring in several poems is a feature of great importance in the poetic quality of *Shih Ching*. Upon this basis, I read poem 196 as one of the unequivocal expressions of the filial desire to return, although "the parent" is not stated in such precise diction as in other poems with comparable thematic imports. The first part of the poem follows:

(1) 宛彼鳴鳩，翰飛戾天。*wan pi ming chiu, han fei li t'ien.*
　　我心憂傷，念昔先人；*wo hsin yu shang, nien hsi hsien jen;*
　　明發不寐，有懷二人。*ming fa pu mei, yu huai erh jen.*　　5–6

[42]Chu Hsi denotes the third stanza of poem 192 as *fu* (*Shih chi-chuan*, XI, 17b) on account of an apparent view to the overall projection. The bird motif occurs at the end of the stanza without obvious metaphorical or narrative connection with the precedent lines. It could easily be argued into a *hsing*.

[43]"On the Possibility of Criticizing Old English Poetry," p. 101.

(1) Small is that singing turtledove:
   It flies up, reaching the sky.
   My heart is grieved and pained,
   Thinking of my ancestors in the past;
   The day breaks: I cannot sleep;   5
   I think with love of the two.

"The two" definitely refers to the parents. I am certain of this interpretation first on account of the occurrence of the birds of the filial return, the turtledove in the quoted stanza and the wagtail and the hawfinch in the rest of the poem—the latter two also respectively substantiate two stanzas of the *hsing* interest; second, because of the mention of the "ancestors in the past" in line 4; and lastly, because of the metaphorical intensification of the thought of the parents by the contexts throughout the poem.

Every bird in such a poem expressive of the filial return is deprived of its ornithological distinction. The bird is a spectral fusion of all birds similarly positioned, including itself. In the art of composition by themes, the cognitive elements of a bird like the bustard in poem 121 is leveled to the extent that it may be substituted by any other bird, as it is by the turtledove again in poem 162, which reveals the same intent with the same effects. We can compare poem 121 with the two passages involving the "Bird of the Filial Return" from poem 162.[44]

Poem 121

(1) 蕭蕭鴇羽，集于苞栩。   *su su pao yü, chi yü pao hsü.*
   王事靡盬：   *wang shih mi ku:*
   不能蓺稷黍，父母何怙？   *pu neng yi chi shu, fu mu ho hu?*
   悠悠蒼天，曷其有所？   *yu yu ts'ang t'ien, ho ch'i yu suo?*   6–7

(2) 蕭蕭鴇翼，集于苞棘。   *su su pao yi, chi yü pao chi.*
   王事靡盬：   *wang shih mi ku:*
   不能蓺黍稷，父母何食？   *pu neng yi shu chi, fu mu ho shih?*
   悠悠蒼天，曷其有極？   *yu yu ts'ang t'ien, ho ch'i yu chi?*   13–14

(3) 蕭蕭鴇行，集于苞桑。   *su su pao hang, chi yü pao sang.*
   王事靡盬：   *wang shih mi ku:*

[44]For a complete analysis of the formulas and themes in poem 162, see Appendix B.

不能蓺稻粱，父母何嘗？ *pu neng yi tao liang, fu mu ho ch'ang?*
悠悠蒼天，曷其有常？ *yu yu ts'ang t'ien, ho ch'i yu ch'ang?* 20–21

(1) Heavily flapping are the bustards' plumes:
   They have perched on the oak trees.
   The king's business never ends:
   I cannot plant my cooking-millet, my wine-millet;
   What can my father and mother rely on?   5
   O you blue Heaven far far away,
   Is there a day when all this will settle?

(2) Heavily flapping are the bustards' wings:
   They have perched on the thorn bushes.
   The king's business never ends: 10
   I cannot plant my wine-millet, my cooking-millet;
   What can my father and mother eat?
   O you blue Heaven far far away,
   Is there a day when all this will end?

(3) Heavily flapping are the bustards in row: 15
   They have perched on the mulberry trees.
   The king's business never ends:
   I cannot plant my rice my spiked millet;
   How can my father and mother have a taste?
   O you blue Heaven far far away,
   Is there a day when everything will have its good, old way?

Stanzas 2 and 3 of poem 162 are almost entirely the same in structural and imagistic patterns as every stanza of poem 121: (1) the
bird in flight; (2) the bird perches on the tree; (3) the king's
business is such and such; and (4) a thought about the parents:

Poem 162

(1) 四牡騑騑，周道倭遲。 *szu mu fei fei, chou tao wo ch'ih.*
   豈不懷歸？ *ch'i pu huai kuei?*
   王事靡盬：我心傷悲。 *wang shih mi ku, wo hsin shang pei.*   4–5

(2) 四牡騑騑，嘽嘽駱馬。 *szu mu fei fei, t'an t'an lo ma.*
   豈不懷歸？ *ch'i pu huai kuei?*
   王事靡盬：不遑啓處。 *wang shih mi ku, pu huang ch'i ch'u*   9–10

(3) 翩翩者雛，載飛載下， *p'ien p'ien che chui, tsai fei tsai hsia,*
集于苞栩。 *chi yü pao hsü.*
王事靡盬：不遑將父。 *wang shih mi ku, pu huang chiang fu.* 14–15

(4) 翩翩者雛，載飛載止， *p'ien p'ien che chui, tsai fei tsai chih,*
集于苞杞。 *chi yü pao ch'i.*
王事靡盬：不遑將母。 *wang shih mi ku, pu huang chiang mu.* 19–20

(5) 駕彼四駱，載驟駸駸。 *chia pi szu lo, tsai chou ch'in ch'in.*
豈不懷歸？ *ch'i pu huai kuei?*
是用作歌，將母來諗。 *shih yung tso ko, chiang mu lai shen.* 24–25

(1) My four steeds gallop without stop;
 The roads of Chou are tortuous and long.
 Do I not long to go home?
 The king's business never ends:
 My heart is sick and sad.

(2) My four steeds run without stop; 5
 They pant, the white stallions with black manes.
 Do I not long to go home?
 The king's business never ends:
 I have no time to rest, or to sit. 10

(3) Agilely fluttering are the turtledoves:
 Now they fly up, now they sink;
 They have perched on the oak trees.
 The king's business never ends:
 I have no time to support my father. 15

(4) Agilely fluttering are the turtledoves:
 Now they fly, now they halt;
 They have perched on the boxthorn bushes.
 The king's business never ends:
 I have no time to support my mother. 20

(5) I yoke the white steeds four, all with black manes,
 And I gallop swiftly, gallop so swiftly.
 Do I not long to go home?
 That is why I have made the song,
 To tell my wish to support my mother. 25

The bustard and the turtledove commence, enrich, and interpret the emotive elements in the individual passages expressive of filial piety and the desire to return to fulfill it. Each passage involving the bird also enriches the emotive elements in the other passages and eventually reinforces the specific theme which they hold in common, the filial return. A unity of poetic signification is thus achieved, through the fusion of many spectra individually represented by a bird as poetic motif. The totality of associations underlies all the poems that make use of the "Bird of the Filial Return."

FIVE

Conclusion

I have been in search of the compositional art of *Shih Ching*. As stated at the outset, I choose to attend to the literary tropes manifesting the importance of technique rather than to content as experience. At this point, I side philosophically with Mark Schorer who, in an essay on the craft of the novel, articulates the critical significance of "technique as discovery."

Technique is the sole means one has of "discovering, exploring, developing his subject, of conveying its meaning, and, finally, of evaluating it." Schorer refers to the poet being motivated to make and also to the critic being invited to analyze. A modern student of ancient poetry may experience an ancient poet's experience without attending to the latter's technique, but he cannot experience an ancient poet's poetry, the "achieved content," that way. It seems that we are narrowing the definition of literary criticism, but in fact we are widening the field of a discipline, comparative literature, by devoting ourselves to the study of form which defines our critical capacity.

For, when we speak of technique, "we speak of nearly everything." In order to experience the "achieved content" of *Shih Ching* poetry, I have gone a tortuous way, through tabulation, charting, and computerization, to establish the basic statistics concerning the word, the phrase, the line, the stanza, and ultimately the poem. In most cases I avoid generalization. Often when internal evidence is available I try to overlook external evidence. The critical principle I have tried to uphold is that it is better, through grouping and analysis, to let the poem reveal itself in its cultural and linguistic contexts than to resort to the aid of modern anthropological findings to compel the poem to suit our speculation. For this purpose, I have chosen the Parry-Lord methodology of oral-formulaic composition as the general guideline of arguments. In so doing, I may have upset two great, respectable scholarly traditions: the Chinese tradition which sometimes maintains that the *Shih Ching* poems are scriptural, or so deeply involved with ancient historical phenomena that their form and technique as lyrical poetry are of lesser interest; and the Western tradition in which it is doubted whether lyrical poetry merits as much attention as epic in terms of analytical method. However, the preceding chapters may have proved that the use of a Western critical methodology for the study of the poetry of *Shih Ching* can also throw new light on the classical lyricism of China. The application of the Parry-Lord theory about the oral making of the European epics to the Chinese formulaic lyrics helps to push forward the frontier of the developing oral poetics.

The mere array of occasional parallels between two genetically unrelated works from two different cultural traditions does not easily achieve anything significant in literary studies. But, assuming the universality of literary art among all humanity, I believe that the processes of creation at some stages of different cultural traditions are comparable. Influences, sharing of allusions, and cross-breeding of sequels, pertinent as topics of comparative studies among European literatures, have no place in the East-West comparative endeavor unless we are content with dealing only with literature produced in quite recent times. However, as soon as we take the technique as discovery, poems of different geneses and of no direct or indirect influences illuminate each other from new perspectives. The case of Cynewulf, for instance, may become less problematic after the study of a similar Chinese case, where it is shown that lettered poets once had recourse to oral formulas during a "transitional period." At this point I have obviously departed from the assumption of Parry and Lord, the latter's "conviction" to dismiss the concept of a transitional period being clearly stated in *The Singer of Tales*. I join with the majority of scholars of Old English studies to affirm the premise of such a period. On the other hand, by recognizing the convention of composition by themes in *Shih Ching*, I have further considered the intricacy of *hsing*, the focal interest of a time-honored dispute in traditional Chinese poetics. The use of a *hsing* motif is more than closely related to the art of composition by themes. Furthermore, following the Parry-Lord method of tabulating the formulas, together with other information internal and external, I also have lent support to, or questioned and even disproved, some principles of dating and categorizing some *Shih Ching* poems.

The poetry of *Shih Ching* shows clear characteristics and abundant traces of formulaic composition by themes, to an extent comparable in technique with classical Greek and Old English poetry. There was once a time, in China as well as Europe, when to versify was to sing and to sing spontaneously, when to make a poem was to manipulate a professional stock of formulaic phrases, and when the criterion of evaluating a poem was not "originality" but the "totality of associations." Without a sympathetic understanding of that particular mode of creation, it is difficult to experience the "achieved content" of a *Shih Ching* poem. The Parry-Lord critical method of epic analysis has led me to clarify an essential aspect of the aesthetics of classical Chinese lyric poetry. And this study, in turn, shall reciprocate by helping to verify that literary theorem which facilitates our comparing of literatures without genetic relation.

APPENDIX A

WHOLE-VERSE FORMULAS PARTICULAR
TO A GROUP

Some whole-verse formulas are particular to a group; that is, they recur only within a specific division of *Shih Ching*, e.g., the *Feng*, the *H.Ya*, or the *T.Ya* in traditional categorization. There are more whole-verse formulas particular to the group *H.Ya* than to the *Feng*, the latter being evidently songs of various regions. A comparison of this list with the statistics revealed in table 6 (page 49) shows an outstanding character of the *H.Ya* in terms of formulaic composition. There is no whole-verse formula particular to the *Lu sung*.

The numeral in parenthesis following each formula indicates the number of occurrences of that formula in the group. Repetitions of the formula within the same poem are not considered.

I. Formulas Particular to the *Feng* (total 41)

以寫我憂	(2)	之子于歸	(4), including
悠悠我思	(4)	之子歸 in poem 22.	
云誰之思	(2)	子之昌兮	(2)
亦可畏也	(2)	執轡如組	(2)
婉兮孌兮	(2)	隰有栗	(2)
上下其音	(2)	將翱將翔	(2)
駕言出遊	(2)	叔于田	(2), both in the
豈不爾思	(4)	Cheng.	
豈無他人	(3)	叔兮伯兮	(3)
衣錦褧衣	(2)	如三月兮	(2)
有美一人	(2)	靜言思之	(2)
悠悠蒼天	(2)	齊侯之子	(2)
一日不見	(2)	清揚婉兮	(2)

中心是悼　(2)　　　　　不流束薪　(2)

女子有行　(3), all in the　　不流束楚　(2)

  Pei-Yung-Wei　　　　汎彼柏舟　(2)

佩玉將將　(2)　　　　　揚之水　　(3)

匪媒不得　(2)　　　　　與子偕老　(2)

匪斧不克　(2)　　　　　勞心忉忉　(2)

彼其之子　(5)　　　　　六轡在手　(2), both in the

彼姝者子　(2)　　　　　　Ch'in.

不瑕有害　(2)　　　　　魯道有蕩　(2), both in the

不知我者　(2)　　　　　　Ch'i.

II. Formulas Particular to the *H. Ya* (total 55)

鳩彼飛隼　(2)　　　　　射夫既同　(2)

憂心孔疚　(2)　　　　　舍彼有罪　(2)

亦孔之哀　(2)　　　　　朱芾斯皇　(2)

鴛鴦在梁　(2)　　　　　受天之祐　(2)

駕彼四牡　(3)　　　　　鐘鼓既設　(2)

我有嘉賓　(2)　　　　　神之聽之　(2)

我心寫兮　(3)　　　　　昔我往矣　(3)

我獨何害　(2)　　　　　先祖是皇　(2)

豈不懷歸　(3)　　　　　曾孫來止　(2)

交交桑扈　(2)　　　　　大人占之　(2)

翰飛戾天　(2)　　　　　陟彼北山　(2)

旂旐央央　(2)　　　　　寧莫之懲　(2)

君子有酒　(3)　　　　　念我獨兮　(2)

鼓瑟鼓琴　(2)　　　　　報以介福　(3)

今我來思　(2)　　　　　萬福攸同　(2)

載飛載止　(2)　　　　　彼何人斯　(2)

祀子孔明　(2)　　　　　不遑啓處　(2)

哀今之人　(2)　　　　　不遑啓居　(2). All "不遑

以爲酒食　(2)　　　　　　X X" in the *H. Ya.*

以其婦子　(2)

憂我父母　(2)　　　　　不騫不崩　(2)

芸其黃矣　(2)　　　　　不畏于天　(2)

之子于征　(2)　　　　　飄風發發　(2)

四牡騑騑　(2)　　　　　汎汎楊舟　(2)

執訊獲醜　(2)　　　　　翩翩者雕　(2)

戢其大翼　(2)　　　　　凡百君子　(2)

民莫不穀　(3)　　　　　民之訛言　(2)

　　　　　　　　　　　六轡沃若　(2)

無罪無辜　(2)　　　　　和樂且湛　(2)

III. Formulas Particular to the *T. Ya* (total 23)

永言配命　(2)　　　　　瞻卬昊天　(2)
遐不作人　(2)　　　　　倬彼雲漢　(2)
我客戾止　(2)　　　　　天降喪亂　(2). All "天降
吉甫作誦　(2)　　　　　　X X" in the *T. Ya*.
兢兢業業　(2)　　　　　天生烝民　(2). All "天生
孔塡不寧　(2)　　　　　　XX" in the *T. Ya*.
纘戎祖考　(2)　　　　　八鸞將將　(2)
以引以翼　(2)　　　　　媚于天子　(2)
自西徂東　(2)　　　　　不顯其光　(2)
夙夜匪懈　(2)　　　　　福祿攸降　(2)
人亦有言　(4)　　　　　民之攸墍　(2)
是用大諫　(2)　　　　　令聞不已　(2)
小心翼翼　(2)

IV. Formulas Particular to the *Chou S.* (total 10)

誰予小子　(3)　　　　　烝畀祖妣　(2)
爲酒爲醴　(2)　　　　　率見昭考　(2)
子孫保之　(2)　　　　　未堪家多難　(2)
時周之命　(2)　　　　　無競維烈　(2)
實函斯活　(2)　　　　　烈文辟公　(2)

V. Formulas Particular to the *Shang S.* (total 2)

顧予烝嘗　(2)　　　　　湯孫之將　(2)

VI. Formulas Particular to the *Lu S.* (none)

. . . .

APPENDIX B

ANOTHER WAY OF PRESENTING THE POEMS AS FORMULAIC (SAMPLES FROM *H. YA*)

161: 鹿鳴

1.9.17. 呦呦鹿鳴

System: 蕭蕭馬鳴 (179/7)

Related: 雝雝鳴雁 (34/3)
杲杲出日 (62/3)

Note: The system "Reduplicatives Noun" yields a large number of formulaic phrases; see Fa-kao Chou, "Reduplicatives" (*Bibliography*). The system "Reduplicatives Noun Verb" produces very few.

2.(10.18.) 食野之苹 (蒿, 芩)

Note: Compare the rhythm of 1 and 2, 呦呦鹿鳴, 食野之苹 (or 9 and 10; 17 and 18), as a unit with that of 關關雎鳩, 在河之洲 (1/1) and note the imagistic relation to musical instruments in both poems, the one about love and the other friendship.

3.11.19. 我有嘉賓

Whole-verse formula: 175/1,2,3.

System: 我有嘉客 (301)

Note: Following the formula in lines 11 and 19, the 我有—嘉賓 formation is broken but kept "recurrent" as follows: 我有旨酒, 嘉賓式燕以敖; and 我有旨酒, 以燕樂嘉賓之心.

22. 和樂且湛

Whole-verse formula: 164/7.

System: 和樂且孺 (164/6)

Related: 或湛樂飲酒 (205/6)

Note: The phrase in 205/6 is "related" on account of its drinking motif. The formula as it occurs in both poems 161 and 164 is unmistakably generated by the music motif.

162: 四牡

General remarks:

I.   Overall composition by theme: bird—tree—king's service —parents.
Cf. Poems 121, 181, and 187: see "The Bird of the Filial Return," Chapter Four.

II. To better understand "preverbal Gestalt" compare the poem with poems 218, 167, and 169.

III. Nominal flexibility (as characteristic of formulaic composition):
(A)   四牡—駱馬—四駱
(B)   苞栩—苞杞
(C) Compare the turtledove motif that precedes the filial thought with the same that prepares for festivity. Cf. "The Bird of the Filial Return," and "Boating: Sorrow and Joy," Chapter Four.

1.6. 四牡騑騑

Whole-verse formula: 218/5.

System: 四牡業業 (167/4), (206/7)
           四牡騤騤 (167/5), (177/1), (257/2), (260/8)
           四牡翼翼 (167/5), (178/1)
           四牡痯痯 (169/3)
           四牡龐龐 (179/1)
           四牡奕奕 (179/4), (261/2)
           四牡彭彭 (205/3), (260/7)
           四牡蹻蹻 (259/4)

Related:　四牡有驕 (57/3)
　　　　　　良馬四之 (53/1)
　　　　　　四驪濟濟 (105/2)
　　　　　　四馬旣閑 (127/3)
　　　　　　四牡孔阜 (128/2), (179/2), (180/1)
　　　　　　駕彼四駱 (162/5)
　　　　　　駕彼四牡 (167/5), (179/4), (191/7)
　　　　　　比物四驪 (177/2)
　　　　　　四牡脩廣 (177/3)
　　　　　　四牡旣佶 (177/5)
　　　　　　乘其四騏 (178/1)
　　　　　　四黃旣駕 (179/6)
　　　　　　四牡項領 (191/7)
　　　　　　乘其四駱 (214/3)
　　　　　　四騏翼翼 (178/1)

4.9.14.19. 王事靡盬

Whole-verse formula:　121/1,2,3.
　　　　　　　　　　167/3.
　　　　　　　　　　169/1,2,3.
　　　　　　　　　　205/1.

Related: 王事多難 (168/1,4)

Note:　The cluster 王事靡盬, 我心傷悲 repeats exactly in 169/1, expressing the identical contextual meaning.

11.16 翩翩者鵻

Whole-verse formula: 171/4.

System: 蜎蜎者蠋 (156/1)
　　　　皇皇者華 (163/1)
　　　　菁菁者莪 (176/1,2,3)
　　　　蓼蓼者莪 (202/1,2)
　　　　楚楚者茨 (209/1)
　　　　裳裳者華 (214/1,2,3)

Related: 翩彼飛鴞 (299/8)

12.(17.) 載飛載下 (止)

Whole-verse formula: 載飛載止 (183/1)
System: 載飛載揚 (183/2)
   載飛載鳴 (196/4)
   載脂載牽 (39/3)
   載馳載驅 (54/1,), (163/2,3,4,5)
   載笑載言 (58/2)
   載寢載興 (128/3)
   載玄載黃 (154/3)
   載飢載渴 (167/2)
   載渴載飢 (167/6)
   載沉載浮 (176/4)
   載飛載行 (183/2)
   載清載濁 (204/5)
   載號載呶 (220/4)
   載驂載駟 (222/2)
   載震載夙 (245/1)
   載謀載惟 (245/7)
   載生載育 (245/1)
   載燔載烈 (245/7)
   載芟載柞 (290)
   載色載笑 (299/2)

13.18 集于苞栩 (杞)

Whole-verse formula: 121/1; 162/4.
System: 集于灌木 (2/1)
   集于苞棘 (121/2)
   集于苞桑 (121/3)

Related: 集于中澤 (181/2)
   無集于穀 (187/1)
   無集于桑 (187/2)
   無集于栩 (187/3)
   集于泮林 (299/8)
   如集于林 (196/6)

10. 不遑啓處

Whole-verse formula: 167/3.

System: 不遑啓居 (167/1,) (168/4)
   不遑假寐 (197/4)

Related: 莫敢或遑 (19/1)
莫敢遑息 (19/2)
莫敢遑處 (19/3)
征夫遑止 (169/1)
不敢怠遑 (305/4)

Note: The cluster 王事靡盬, 不遑啓處 repeats exactly in 167/3, expressing the identical contextual meaning. The items in the "related" category are all expressive of the hardship of military campaigns.

5. 我心傷悲

Whole-verse formula: 14/3.
167/6.
169/2.
147/2 (我心傷悲兮)

System: 我心憂傷 (146/2), (192/1), (196/1), (197/2)
無使我心悲兮 (159/4)

Note: The cluster 王事靡盬, 我心傷悲 repeats exactly in 169/2, expressing the identical contextual meaning. The items in the "related" category are all expressive of the hardship of military campaigns.

3.8.23. 豈不懷歸

Whole-verse formula: 168/4; 207/1,2,3.

21. 駕彼四駱

System: 駕彼四牡 (167/5)
(179/4)
(191/7)

Note: The nominal flexibility noted in III(A) is best understood with the system in view: 四牡—四駱—四牡

22. 載驟駸駸

System: 載驅薄薄 (105/1)
載穫濟濟 (290)
載弁俅俅 (292)

Note: The system 載 X 載 X (see 12.[17.]) is prolific because the X—X elements, governed and vivified by 載 —載, are easy to substitute. I suspect that it is the 載—載 repetition that invites the singer to rely on the system. In comparison, this system (22.) only involves a 載, but the system (載X Reduplicatives), still, seems to have rescued itself from sterility by repeating its adverbial element, a variant perhaps readily established on the preverbal Gestalt level.

24. 是用作歌

System: 是用孝享 (166/4)
是用不集 (195/3)
是用不得于道 (195/3)
是用不潰于成 (195/4)
是用大諫 (253/5), (254/1)
是用大介 (293)

Related: 我是用憂 (223/8)

SELECTED BIBLIOGRAPHY

PART ONE

Secondary sources in English and other Western languages dealing with
early Chinese poetry, *Shih Ching* in particular, and with classical and
medieval European poetry generally of oral-formulaic interest.

Adams, John F. "The Anglo-Saxon Riddle as Lyric Mode." *Criticism* VII
(1965): 335–348.

Anderson, Warren D. *Ethos and Education in Greek Music.* Cambridge, Mass.,
1966.

Bartlett, A. C. *The Larger Rhetorical Patterns in Anglo-Saxon Poetry.* New York,
1935.

Benson, Larry D. "The Literary Character of Anglo-Saxon Formulaic
Poetry." *PMLA* LXXXI (1966): 334–341.

Bonjour, Adrien, "*Beowulf* and the Beasts of Battle." *PMLA* LXXII (1957):
563–573.

Boodberg, Peter A. "Cedules from a Berkeley Workshop in Asiatic Philology." *THHP* N.S. VII: 2 (1969), 1–38.

Bowra, Cecil Maurice. *Heroic Poetry.* London, 1952.

———. *Primitive Song.* New York, 1962.

Bright, James W. "The 'Ubi Sunt' Formula." *Modern Language Notes* VIII
(1893): 94.

Brodeur, Arthur G. *The Art of Beowulf.* Berkeley, 1959.

Brower, Robert H., and Miner, Earl. *Japanese Court Poetry.* Stanford, 1961.

Campbell, Jackson J. "Oral Poetry in the *Seafarer.*" *Speculum* XXXV (1960):
87–96.

Cassidy, Frederic G. "How Free was the Anglo-Saxon Scop?" *Franciplegius,* edited by Jess B. Bessinger and Robert P. Creed, pp. 75–85. New
York, 1965.

Chadwick, H. M. *The Heroic Age.* 1912. Reprint. Cambridge, 1967.

———, and Chadwick, N. K. *The Growth of Literature.* 3 vols. Cambridge,
1932–1940.

Chadwick, N. K., and Zhirmunsky, Victor. *Oral Epics of Central Asia.*
Cambridge, 1969.

Chambers, R. W. *Beowulf: An Introduction to the Study of the Poem.* With
Supplement by C. L. Wrenn. Cambridge, 1959.

Chang, Kwang-chih. *The Archaeology of Ancient China.* New Haven, 1971.

Chen, Shih-hsiang. "The *Shih Ching:* Its Generic Significance in Chinese
Literary History and Poetics." *BIHP* XXXIX, pt. 1 (1969): 371–413.

———. "In Search of the Beginnings of Chinese Literary Criticism."
Semitic and Oriental Studies XI (1951): 45–64.

———. "Chinese Poetry and Its Popular Sources." N. s. *THHP* II: 2
(1961), 320–326.

Chou, Fa-kao. "Reduplicatives in the *Book of Odes.*" *BIHP* XXXIV, pt.
2 (1963): 661–698.

Chow, Tse-tsung. "The Early History of the Chinese Word *Shih* (poetry)."

Wen-lin: Studies in the Chinese Humanities, edited by Chow Tse-tsung, pp. 151–209. Madison, 1968.

Combellack, Frederic M. "Milman Parry and Homeric Artistry." *Comparative Literature* (Oregon) XI (1959): 193–208.

Creed, Robert P. "Studies in the Techniques of Composition of the Beowulf Poetry in British Museum MS. Cotton Vitellius A XV." Ph. D. dissertation, Harvard University, 1955.

———. "On the Possibility of Criticizing Old English Poetry." *Texas Studies in Literature and Language* III (1961): 97–106.

———. "The Art of the Singer: Three Old English Tellings of the Offering of Isaac." *Old English Poetry,* edited by Robert P. Creed, pp. 69–92. Providence, 1967.

———. "The Making of an Anglo-Saxon Poem." *ELH* XXVI (1959): 445–454.

———. "The Andswarode-System in Old English Poetry." *Speculum* XXXII (1957): 523–528.

———. "The Singer Looks at His Sources." *Comparative Literature* (Oregon) XIV (1962): 44–52.

Crosby, Ruth. "Oral Delivery in the Middle Ages." *Speculum* XI (1936): 88–110.

Crowne, David K. "The Hero on the Beach—an Example of Composition by Theme in Anglo-Saxon Poetry." *Neuphilologische Mitteilungen* LXI (1960): 362–372.

Culley, Robert C. *Oral Formulaic Language in the Biblical Psalms.* Toronto, 1967.

Curschmann, Michael. "Oral Poetry in Medieval English, French and German Literature: Some Notes on Recent Research." *Speculum* XLII (1967): 36–52.

Curtius, Ernst Robert. *European Literature and the Latin Middle Ages.* Translated by Willard R. Trask. New York, 1963.

Damon, Phillip. *Modes of Analogy in Ancient and Medieval Verse.* UCPCP, XV, no. 6. Berkeley, 1961.

Diamond, Robert E. "The Diction of the Signed Poems of Cynewulf." *PQ* XXXVIII (1959): 228–241.

———. "Theme as Ornament in Anglo-Saxon Poetry." *PMLA* LXXVI (1961): 461–468.

Dobson, W.A.C.H. "Linguistic Evidence and the Dating of the *Book of Songs.*" *T'oung Pao* LI (1964): 322–334.

———. "The Origin and Development of Prosody in Early Chinese Poetry." *T'oung Pao* LIV, (1968): 231–250.

———. *The Language of the Book of Songs.* Toronto, 1968.

Dudbridge, Glen. *The Hsi-yu chi: A Study of Antecedents to the Sixteenth-Century Chinese Novel.* Cambridge, 1971.

Duggan, Joseph J. "Formulas in the *Couronnement de Louis.*" *Romania* LXXXVII (1966): 315–344.

———. *The Song of Roland: Formulaic Style and Poetic Craft.* Berkeley, 1973.

Emeneau, M. B. "Toda Dream Songs." *Journal of the American Oriental Society* XXCV (1965): 39–44.

Finlayson, John. "Formulaic Technique in *Morte Arthure.*" *Anglia* LXXXI (1963): 327–393.

Frankel, Hans H. "The Formulaic Language of the Chinese Ballad 'Southeast Fly the Peacocks.'" *BIHP* XXXIX (1969): 219–244.

Fry, Donald K. "Aesthetic Application of Oral-Formulaic Theory: *Judith* 199–216a." Ph.D. dissertation, University of California, Berkeley, 1966.

———. "Old English Formulas and Systems." *English Studies* XLVIII (1967): 193–204.

———. Old English Oral-Formulaic Themes and Type-Scenes." *Neophilologus* LII (1968): 48–54.

———. "Themes and Type-Scenes in *Elene* 1–113." *Speculum* XLIV (1969): 35–45.

———. "Some Aesthetic Implications of a New Definition of the Formula." *Neuphilologische Mitteilungen* LXIX (1968): 561–522.

———. "The Hero on the Beach in *Finnsburh*." *Neuphilologische Mitteilungen* LXVII (1966): 27–31.

———. "The Heroine on the Beach in *Judith*." *Neuphilologische Mitteilungen* LXVIII (1967): 168–184.

Greenfield, Stanley B. "The Exile-Wanderer in Anglo-Saxon Poetry." Ph.D. dissertation, University of California, Berkeley, 1950.

———. "The Formulaic Expression of the Theme of 'Exile' in Anglo-Saxon Poetry." *Speculum* XXX (1955): 200–206.

———. "The Canons of Old English Criticism." *ELH* XXXIV (1967): 141–155.

———. "Syntactic Analysis and Old English Poetry." *Neuphilologische Mitteilungen* LXIV (1963): 373–378.

———. "Grendel's Approach to Heorot: Syntax and Poetry." *Old English Poetry*, edited by Robert P. Creed, pp. 275–284. Providence, 1967.

Hainsworth, J. B. *The Flexibility of the Homeric Formula*. Oxford, 1968.

Havelock, Eric A. *Preface to Plato*. Cambridge, Mass., 1963.

Hightower, James Robert. *Han Shih Wai Chuan*. Cambridge, Mass., 1952.

———. "The *Han-shih Wai-chuan* and the *San Chia Shih*." *Harvard Journal of Asiatic Studies* XI: 3–4 (1948), 241–310.

———. "Chinese Literature in the Context of World Literature." *Comparative Literature* (Oregon), V (1953): 117–124.

Hsü, Cho-yün. *Ancient China in Transition*. Stanford, 1965.

Hung, William, et al., eds. *A Concordance to Shih Ching*. Harvard-Yenching Sinological Index Series, Supplement No. 9. Peking, 1934.

Irving, Edward B., Jr. "Image and Meaning in the Elegies." *Old English Poetry*, edited by Robert P. Creed, pp. 153–166. Providence, 1967.

Karlgren, Bernhard. *Glosses on the Book of Odes*. Stockholm, 1946.

———. *Grammata Serica*. Reprint. Taipei, 1966.

———. "*Shi King* Researches." *Bulletin of the Museum of Far Eastern Antiquities* IV (1932): 117–185.

———. *The Book of Odes*. Stockholm, 1950.

Kellogg, R. L. "The South Germanic Oral Tradition." *Franciplegius*, edited by Jess B. Bessinger and Robert P. Creed, pp. 66–74. New York, 1965.

Kennedy, George A. *Selected Works*. Edited by Tien-yi Li. New Haven, 1964.

Kirk, G. S. *Homer and the Epic*. Cambridge, 1965.

Lawrence, R. F. "The Formulaic Theory and Its Application to English Alliterative Poetry." *Essays on Style and Language,* edited by Roger Fowler, pp. 166–183. London, 1966.

Leach, MacEdward. "Problems of Collecting Oral Literature." *PMLA* LXXVII (1962): 335–340.

Legge, James. *The Book of Poetry.* Shanghai, n.d.

Leslie, R. F. "*The Wanderer*: Theme and Structure." *Old English Literature,* edited by Martin Stevens and Jerome Mandel, pp. 139–162. Lincoln, Nebraska, 1968.

Lewis, C. S. "The Anthropological Approach." *English and Medieval Studies Presented to J.R.R. Tolkien,* edited by Norman Davis and C. L. Wrenn, pp. 219–230. London, 1962.

———. *Preface to Paradise Lost.* London, 1942.

Liu, James J. Y. *The Art of Chinese Poetry.* Chicago, 1966.

Lord, Albert B. "Homer and Huso I: The Singer's Rests in Greek and South Slavic Heroic Song." *TPAPA* LXVII (1936): 106–113.

———. "Homer and Huso II: Narrative Inconsistencies in Homer and Oral Poetry." *TPAPA* LXIX (1938): 439–445.

———. "Homer and Huso III: Enjambment in Greek and South Slavic Heroic Song." *TPAPA* LXXIX (1949): 113–124.

———. "Homer, Parry, and Huso." *American Journal of Archaeology* LII (1948): 34–44.

———. "Yugoslav Epic Folk Poetry." *Journal of the International Folk Music Council* III (1951): 57–61.

———. "Composition by Theme in Homer and South Slavic Epos." *TPAPA* LXXXIII (1952): 71–80.

———. "Homer's Originality: Oral Dictated Texts." *TPAPA* LXXXIV (1953): 124–134.

———. "Beowulf and Odysseus." *Franciplegius,* edited by Jess B. Bessinger and Robert P. Creed. New York, 1965.

———. *The Singer of Tales.* Cambridge, Mass., 1964.

Loon, Piet van der. *Register Zum Shih Ching.* Leiden, 1943.

Magoun, Francis P., Jr. "Oral-Formulaic Character of Anglo-Saxon Narrative Poetry." *Speculum* XXVIII (1953): 446–467.

———. "The Theme of the Beasts of Battle in Anglo-Saxon Poetry." *Neuphilologische Mitteilungen* LVI (1955): 81–90.

———. "Bede's Story of Caedmon: the Case History of an Anglo-Saxon Oral Singer." *Speculum* XXX (1955): 49–63.

———. "Two Verses in the Old English *Waldere* Characteristic of Oral Poetry." *Beiträge zur Geschichte der deutschen Sprache und Literatur* (Tübingen) LXXX (1958): 214–218.

Mattos, Gilbert L. "Tonal 'Anomalies' in the *Kuo Feng Odes*." *THHP* N. S. IX: 1,2 (1971), 306–325.

McNaughton, William. *The Book of Songs.* Twayne's World Authors Series, 77. New York, 1971.

———. "The Composite Image: *Shy Jing* Poetics." *Journal of the American Oriental Society* LXXXIII (1963): 92–103.

Metcalf, Allan. "The Natural Animals in *Beowulf*." *Neuphilologische Mitteilungen* LXIV (1963): 378–389.

Miner, Earl. *An Introduction to Japanese Court Poetry.* Stanford, 1968.

————. "Formula: Japanese and Western Evidence Compared." Paper read in the 5th International Congress of the International Comparative Literature Association in Belgrade, 1967.

Mustanoja, Tauno F. "The Presentation of Ancient Germanic Poetry— Looking for Parallels (a Note on the Presentation of Finnish Runos)." *Neuphilologische Mitteilungen* LX (1959): 1–11.

————. "The Unnamed Woman's Song of Mourning over Beowulf and the Tradition of Ritual Lamentation." *Neuphilologische Mitteilungen* LXVIII (1967): 1–27.

Nagler, Michael N. "Formula and Motif in the Homeric Epics: Prolegomena to an Aesthetics of Oral Poetry." Ph. D. dissertation, University of California, Berkeley, 1966.

————. "Towards a Generative View of the Oral Formula." *TPAPA* XCVIII (1967): 269–311.

Nichols, Stephen G., Jr. *Formulaic Diction and Thematic Composition in the Chanson de Roland*. University of North Carolina Studies in the Romance Languages and Literature, 36. Chapel Hill, 1961.

Nicholson, John Edward. "Oral Techniques in the Compoistion of Expanded Anglo-Saxon Verses." *PMLA* LXXVII (1963): 287–292.

Notopoulos, James A. "Mnemosyne in Oral Literature." *TPAPA* LXIX (1938): 465–493.

O'Neil, Wayne A. "Oral-Formulaic Structure in Old English Elegiac Poetry." Ph.D. dissertation, University of Wisconsin, 1960.

————. "Another Look at Oral Poetry in the *Seafarer*." *Speculum* XXXV (1960): 596–600.

Parry, Milman. *L'Épithète traditionnelle dans Homère*. Paris, 1928.

————. *The Making of Homeric Verse: The Collected Papers of Milman Parry*. Edited by Adam Parry. Oxford, 1971.

————. "Studies in the Epic Technique of Oral Verse-making, I: Homer and Homeric Style." *HSCP* XLI (1930): 73–147.

————. "Studies in the Epic Technique of Oral Verse-making, II: The Homeric Language as the Language of Oral Poetry." *HSCP* XLIII (1932): 1–50.

————. "Whole Formulaic Verses in Greek and Southslavic Heroic Poetry." *TPAPA* LXIV (1933): 179–197.

————. and Lord, Albert B. *Serbo-Croatian Heroic Songs*. 2 vols. Cambridge, Mass. and Belgrade, 1954.

Pound, Ezra, *The Confucian Odes*. New York, 1959.

Ramsey, Lee Carter. "The Theme of Battle in Old English Poetry." Ph.D. dissertation, Indiana University, 1965.

Renoir, Alain. "*Judith* and the Limits of Poetry." *English Studies* XLIII (1962): 145–155.

————. "Point of View and Design for Terror in *Beowulf*." *Neuphilologische Mitteilungen* LXIII (1962): 154–167.

————. "The Heroic Oath in *Beowulf*, the *Chanson de Roland*, and the *Nibelungenlied*." *Studies in Old English Literature in Honor of Arthur G. Brodeur*, edited by Stanley B. Greenfield, pp. 237–266. Eugene, 1963.

————. "Oral-Formulaic Theme Survival—A Possible Instance in the *Nibelungenlied*." *Neuphilologische Mitteilungen* LXV (1964): 70–75.

Rogers, H. L. "The Crypto-Psychological Character of the Oral Formula." *English Studies* XLVII (1966): 89–102.

Ross, James. "Formulaic Composition in Gaelic Oral Literature." *MP* LVII (1959): 1–12.

Schaar, Claes. *Critical Studies in the Cynewulf Group*. Lund Studies in English, 17. Lund, 1949.

————. "On a New Theory of Old English Poetic Diction." *Neophilologus* XL (1956): 301–305.

Schafer, Edward H. *The Vermilion Bird*. Berkeley, 1967.

Scholes, Robert, and Kellogg, Robert. *The Nature of Narrative*. Oxford, 1966.

Schorer, Mark. "Technique as Discovery." *Approaches to the Novel*, edited by Robert Scholes, pp. 141–160. San Francisco, 1966.

Serruys, Paul L. M. "The Function and Meaning of *yün* 云 in *Shih Ching* —Its Cognates and Variants." *Monumenta Serica* XXIX (1970–1971): 264–337.

Slay, D. "Some Aspects of the Technique of Composition of Old English Verse," *Transactions of the Philological Society*, London, 673 [1952], 1–14. Oxford, 1953.

Speirs, John. *Medieval English Poetry: the Non-Chaucerian Tradition*. London, 1957.

Stevick, Robert D. "The Oral-Formulaic Analyses of Old English Verse." *Speculum* XXXVII (1962): 382–389.

————. "The Text and the Composition of *The Seafarer*." *PMLA* LXXX (1965): 332–336.

Tatlock, John S. P. "Layamon's Poetic Style and Its Relations." *The Manly Anniversary Studies in Language and Literature*, pp. 3–11. Chicago, 1923.

————. and Kennedy, Arthur. "Epic Formulas, Especially in Layamon." *PMLA* XXXVIII (1923): 494–529.

Taylor, Paul Beekman. "Themes of Death in *Beowulf*." *Old English Poetry*, edited by Robert P. Creed, pp. 249–274. Providence, 1967.

Tolkien, J.R.R. "*Beowulf*: the Monsters and the Critics." *Proceedings of the British Academy* XXII (1936): 245–295.

Waldron, Ronald A. "Oral-Formulaic Technique and Middle English Alliterative Poetry." *Speculum* XXXII (1957): 792–804.

Waley, Arthur. *The Book of Songs*. New York, 1960.

Waterbury, Florence. *Bird-deities in China*. *Artibut Asiae Supplementum*, 10. Artibus Asiae, 1952.

Watts, Ann Chalmers. *The Lyre and the Harp*. New Haven, 1969.

Whallon, William. "The Diction of *Beowulf*." *PMLA* LXXVI (1961): 309–319.

————. "Formulas for Heroes in the *Iliad* and in *Beowulf*." *MP* LXIII (1965): 95–104.

————. *Formula, Character and Context: Studies in Homeric, Old English and Old Testament Poetry*. Washington, D.C., 1969.

Whitelock, Dorothy. *The Audience of Beowulf*. Oxford, 1951.

————, ed. *The Anglo-Saxon Chronicle*. New Brunswick, N.J., 1961.

Wrenn, C. L. *A Study of Old English Literature*. New York, 1967.

Will, Frederic. "Palamas, Lorca, and a Perspective for Comparative Literature." *Comparative Literature Studies* I:2 (1964), 133–142.

Yip, Wai-lim. *Ezra Pound's Cathay*. Princeton, 1969.

PART TWO

Chinese and Japanese sources. Standard works established before the T'ang, e.g., *Tso Chuan, Shih chi,* and the *Cheng commentaries* on *Shih Ching,* are not listed.

Chang, Hsi-t'ang (張西堂). *Shih Ching liu lun* (詩經六論). Peking, 1957.

Chang, Shou-yung (張壽鏞). *Shih-shih ch'u-kao* (詩史初稿). n.p., 1942.

Ch'en, Huan (陳奐). *Shih Mao-shih-chuan shu* (詩毛氏傳疏). Reprint. Taipei, 1968.

Ch'en, Meng-chia (陳夢家). *"Ku wen-tzu chung chih Shang Chou chi-szu"* (古文字中之商周祭祀). *YCHP* XIX (1936): 91–155.

———. *"Kao-mei chiao-she tsu-miao t'ung-k'ao"* (高禖郊社祖廟通考). *THHP* XII (1937): 445–472.

Ch'en, P'an (陳槃). *"Ku she-hui t'ien-shou yü chi-szu chih kuan-hsi"* (古社會田狩與祭祀之關係). *Chung-kuo k'o-hsüeh yüan shih-yü-suo chi-k'an* XXI: 1(1949), 1–17.

Chen, Shih-hsiang (陳世驤). *"Chung-kuo shih chih chih yüan-shih kuan-nien shih-lun"* (中國詩字之原始觀念試論). *BIHP* supplement 4 (1961): 899–912.

Ch'en, Tzu-chan (陳子展). *Ya sung hsüan-yi* (雅頌選譯). Hong Kong, 1966.

Ch'en, Ying-t'ang (陳應棠). *Mao-shih hsün-ku hsin-cheng* (毛詩訓詁新證). Taipei, 1969.

Ch'eng, T'i-hsien (成惕軒). *"Shih Ching chung te ping yü nung"* (詩經中的兵與農). *Kuo-li Cheng-chih ta-hsüeh hsüeh-pao* I (1960): 193–218.

Cheng, Tien (鄭奠) and Mai Mei-ch'iao (麥梅翹), eds. *Ku-han-yü yü-fa tzu-liao hui-pien* (古漢語語法資料彙編). Peking, 1965.

Ch'i, Szu-ho (齊思和). "Mao-shih ku ming k'ao" (毛詩穀名考). *YCHP* XXXVI (1949): 263–311.

Chia, Tsu-chang (賈祖璋). *Niao yü wen-hsüeh* (鳥與文學). Shanghai, 1931.

Chia, Tsu-chang (賈祖璋) and Chia Tsu-shan (賈祖珊). *Chung-kuo chih-wu t'u-chien* (中國植物圖鑑). Peking, 1955.

Chiang Shan-kuo (蔣善國). *San-pai-p'ien yen-lun* (三百篇演論). Taipei, 1966.

Chiao, Hsün (焦循). *Mao-shih pu-shu* (毛詩補疏). Reprint. Canton, 1829.

Ch'ien, Chung-shu (錢鍾書). *T'an yi lu* (談藝錄). Hong Kong, 1968.

Chow, Tse-tsung (周策縱). *P'o fu hsin-ku* (破斧新詁). Singapore, 1969.

———. *"Chuan o k'ao"* (卷阿考). N.s *THHP* VII: 2 (1969), 176–205.

Chu, Hsi (朱熹). *Shih chi-chuan* (詩集傳). Reprint. Taipei, 1967.

Chu, Tung-jun (朱東潤). *Tu Shih szu-lun* (讀詩四論). Shanghai, n.d.

Chu, Tzu-ch'ing (朱自清). *Shih-yen-chih pien* (詩言志辨). Reprint. Taipei, 1954.

Ch'ü, Wan-li (屈萬里). *Shih Ching shih-yi* (詩經釋義). Reprint. Taipei, 1967.

———. *"Lun Kuo feng fei min-chien ko-yao te pen-lai mien-mu"* (論國風非民間歌謠的本來面目). *BIHP* XXXIV: 2 (1963), 477–504.

———. *"Lun Ch'u chü chih shih chu-ch'eng te shih-tai"* (論出車之詩著成的時代). *THHP* N.s. I: 2 (1957), 102–110.

Chung, Ching-wen (鍾敬文), ed. *Min-chien wen-yi hsin-lun chi* (民間文藝新論集). Peking, 1950.

Fang, Yü-jun (方玉潤). *Shih Ching yüan shih* (詩經原始). Reprint. Taipei, 1950.

Fu, Szu-nien (傅斯年). *Fu Meng-chen hsien-sheng chi* (傅孟眞先生集). Taipei, 1951.

Fukuda, Fukuichirō (福田福一郎), ed. *Shikyō ikku sakuin* (詩經一句索引). Tokyo, 1931.

Hao, Ching (郝敬). *Mao-shih yüan-chieh* (毛詩原解). Reprint. 1891.

Ho, K'ai (賀凱). "*Shih Ching chung te ch'ung-yen ho lien-mien-tz'u te fen-ho yün-yung*" (詩經中的重言和連綿詞的分合運用). *Shan-hsi shih-fan hsüeh-yüan hsüeh-pao* III (1959): 43–51.

Ho, Ping-ti (何炳棣). *Huang-t'u yü Chung-kuo nung-yeh te ch'i-yüan* (黃土與中國農業的起源). Hong Kong, 1969.

Ho, Ting-sheng (何定生). *Shih Ching chin-lun* (詩經今論). Taipei, 1968.

Hsieh, Chin-ch'ing (謝晉青). *Shih Ching chih nü-hsing te yen-chiu* (詩經之女性的研究). Shanghai, 1924.

Hsieh, Wu-liang (謝无量). *Shih Ching yen-chiu* (詩經研究). Hong Kong, 1959.

Hsu, Cho-yün (許倬雲). "*Chou-jen te hsing-ch'i chi Chou-wen-hua te chi-ch'u*" (周人的興起及周文化的基礎). *BIHP* XXXVIII (1968): 435–458.

Hsü, Fu-kuan (徐復觀). "*Feng-chien cheng-chih she-hui te peng-k'ui chi tien-hsing chuan-chih cheng-chih te ch'eng-li*" (封建政治社會的崩潰及典型專制政治的成立). *Hsin-ya shu-yüan hsüeh-shu nien-k'an* XI (1969): 43–107.

Hu, P'u-an (胡樸安). *Shih Ching hsüeh* (詩經學). Shanghai, n. d.

Hung, Yeh (洪業). "*P'o fu*" (破斧). *THHP* N.S. I: 1 (1956), 21–62.

Juan, Yüan (阮元). *Mao-shih chiao-k'an chi* (毛詩校戡記). Reprint. Canton, 1829.

Jen-min wen-hsüeh ch'u-pan-she pien-chi-pu (人民文學出版社編輯部), ed. *Shih Ching yen-chiu lun-wen-chi* (詩經研究論文集). Peking, 1959.

Kao, Pao-kuang (高葆光). *Shih Ching hsin p'ing-chia* (詩經新評價). Taichung, 1969.

Kojima, Kentarō (兒島獻吉郎), *Moshi Soji kō* (毛詩楚辭考). Translated by Sui Shu-shen (隋樹森). Shanghai, 1936.

Ku, Chieh-kang (顧頡剛), ed. *Ku shih pien* (古史辨). Vol. III. Peking, 1931.

———. "*Shang wang-kuo te shih-mo*" (商王國的始末). *Wen-shih tsa-chih* I: 2 (1941), 1–8.

———. "*Chou-jen te chüeh-ch'i chi ch'i k'e Shang*" (周人的崛起及其克商). *Wen-shih tsa-chih* I: 3 (1941), 8–16.

Ku, Yen-wu (顧炎武). *Jih chih lu* (日知錄). Reprint. Shanghai, 1935.

———. *Shih pen-yin* (詩本音). Reprint. 1885.

K'ung, Kuang-shen (孔廣森). *Shih sheng-lei* (詩聲類). Reprint. 1924.

K'ung Ying-ta (孔穎達). *Mao-shih cheng-yi* (毛詩正義). *SPPY*. Reprint. Taipei, 1967.

———. *Shang Shu cheng-yi* (尚書正義). *SSCCS*. Reprint. Taipei, 1963.

Lai, Yen-yüan (賴炎元). *Han-shih wai-chuan k'ao-cheng* (韓詩外傳考徵). Taipei, 1963.

Li, Ch'ao-sun (李超孫). *Shih shih-tsu k'ao* (詩氏族考). Reprint. Shanghai, 1936.

Liang, Ch'i-ch'ao (梁啓超). "*Shih szu-shih ming-yi*" (釋四詩名義). *Chung-kuo wen-hsüeh yen-chiu*, edited by Cheng Chen-to. Shanghai, 1927.

Liu, Chieh (劉節). *Ku-shih k'ao ts'un* (古史考存). Reprint. Hong Kong, 1963.

Liu, Ch'iu-ch'ao (劉秋潮). "*Feng-shih te ch'i-chü*" (風詩的起句). *Ta-lu tsa-chih* XII (1956): 79–80.

Liu, Shih-p'ei (劉師培). *Mao-shih tz'u-li chü-yao* (毛詩詞例舉要). Reprint. Taipei, 1960.

Lu, Chi (陸璣). *Mao-shih ts'ao-mu-niao-shou-ch'ung-yü shu* (毛詩草木鳥獸蟲魚疏). Reprint. Hong Kong, 1967.

Lu, Wen-yü (陸文郁). *Shih ts'ao-mu chin-shih* (詩草木今釋). Tientsin, 1957.

Ma, Jui-ch'en (馬瑞辰). *Mao-shih chuan-chien t'ung-shih* (毛詩傳箋通釋)· *SPPY*. Reprint. Taipei, 1968.

Matsumoto, Massaki (松本雅明). *Shikyō shohen no seiritsu ni kansuru kenkyu* (詩經諸篇の成立し關する研究). *Tōyō-bunko runso*, 41. Tokyo, 1958.

Ogawa, Tamaki (小川環樹). *Shikyō ibun no oninteki tokuchō*" (詩經異文の音樂的特徵). *Ritsumeikan bungaku* V: 6 (1960), 367–391.

Oka, Gempō (岡元鳳). *Moshi hinbutsu zukō* (毛詩品物圖考). Reprint. Taipei, 1967.

Ou-yang, Hsiu (歐陽修). *Shih pen-yi* (詩本義). *SPTK*. Reprint. Shanghai, n. d.

Pai, Tun-jen (白惇仁). *Shih Ching yin-yüeh wen-hsüeh k'ao* (詩經音樂文學考)· Taipei, 1970.

P'i, Hsi-jui (皮錫瑞). *Ching-hsüeh t'ung-lun* (經學通論). Reprint. Hong Kong, 1961.

P'i, Shu-min (皮述民). "*Yi-shih k'ao-pien*" (逸詩考辨). *Kuo-li Cheng-chih ta-hsüeh hsüeh-pao* XI (1965): 117–164.

Shirakawa, Shizuka (白川靜). "*Shih Ching li-shuo*" (詩經蠡說). *BIHP* supplement 4 (1960): 83–103.

———. "*Shūhan no seiritsu*" (周頌の成立). *Ritsumeikan bungaku* V: 6 (1960), 392–414.

T'ang, kuei-chang (唐圭璋). *Sung tz'u hu-chien k'ao* (宋詞互見考). Taipei, 1971.

T'ang, Lan (唐蘭). "*Pu-tz'u shih-tai te wen-hsüeh ho pu-tz'u wen-hsüeh*" (卜辭時代的文學和卜辭文學). *THHP* XI: 3 (1936), 657–702.

Ting, Chu-yün (丁竹筠). *Mao-shih cheng-yün* (毛詩正韻). Reprint. n.p. 1924.

Ting, Wei-fen (丁惟汾). *Ku-ya-t'ang ts'ung-shu liu-chung* (詁雅堂叢書六種). Reprint. Taipei, 1966.

Ts'en, Chung-mien (岑仲勉). *Liang Chou wen-shih lun ts'ung* (兩周文史論叢). Shanghai, 1958.

Ts'ui, Shu (崔述). *Ts'ui Tung-pi yi-shu* (崔東壁遺書). Reprint. Shanghai, 1936.

Tung, Tso-pin (董作賓). "*Wu-wang fa Chou nien-yüeh-jih chin k'ao*" (武王伐紂年月日今考). In *Tung Tso-pin hsüeh-shu lun-chu*. Taipei, 1962.

———. *Yin li p'u* (殷曆譜). *BIHP* special 23 (1945).

Tung, T'ung-ho (董同龢), trans. *Kao Pen-han Shih Ching chu-shih* (高本漢詩經注釋). Taipei, 1960.

Wang, Ching-chih (王靜芝). *Shih Ching-t'ung-shih* (詩經通釋). Taipei, 1968.

Wang, Chung (汪中). *Shu-hsüeh pu-yi* (述學補遺). *SPTK*. Reprint. Shanghai, n. d.

Wang, Fu-chih (王夫之). *Shih kuang-chuan* (詩廣傳). Reprint. Peking, 1965.

Wang, Kuo-wei (王國維). *Wang Kuan-t'ang hsien-sheng ch'üan-chi* (王觀堂先生全集). Taipei, 1968.

Wang, Hsien-ch'ien (王先謙). *Shih san-chia-yi chi-shu* (詩三家義集疏). Reprint. Taipei, 1957.

Wang, Yin-chih (王引之). *Ching-yi shu-wen* (經義述聞). Reprint. Taipei, 1956.

Wen, I-to (聞一多). *Wen I-to ch'üan-chi* (聞一多全集). Shanghai, 1948.

Wu, K'ai-sheng (吳闓生). *Shih-yi hui-t'ung* (詩義會通). Hong Kong, 1961.

Yang, Shen (楊愼). *Feng ya yi-p'ien* (風雅逸篇). Reprint. Shanghai, 1939.

Yao, Chi-heng (姚際恒). *Shih Ching t'ung-lun* (詩經通論). Reprint. Hong Kong, 1963.

Yen, Ts'an (嚴粲). *Shih ch'i* (詩緝). Reprint. Taipei, 1950.

Yoshikawa, Kōjirō (吉川幸次郎). *Shikyō Kokufū* (詩經國風). in *Yoshikawa Kōjirō Zenshū*. Tokyo, 1969.

Yü, Ching-jang (于景讓). "*Ch'ang-ti yü t'ang-ti*" (常棣與唐棣). *Ta-lu tsa-chih* XXI, (1960): 205–209.

Yü, Kuan-ying (余冠英). *Shih Ching hsüan chu* (詩經選注). Reprint. Hong Kong, 1966.

Yu, Kuo-en (游國恩). *Hsien Ch'in wen-hsüeh* (先秦文學). Reprint. Hong Kong, 1965.

Yü, P'ing-po (俞平伯). "*Shih te ko yü sung*" (詩的歌與誦). *THHP* IX (1934): 611–630.

Yü, T'ing-lun (俞廷掄), ed. *Shih Ching yüeh-p'u* (詩經樂譜). Reprint. Shanghai, 1937.

INDEX OF POEMS

NOTE: *Pages on which a poem has
been quoted have been italicized.*

INDEX

Acoustic pattern, 35, 51, 52, 54
Adjectival reduplicatives, 70
Allegorism, 1, 6
Anglo-Saxon poetry, 38, 89, 103, 107.
    See also Old-English poetry
Aster-gathering motif, 9, 10, 55–56, 81,
    115–116

Beast of Battle theme, 20, 21, 24, 100,
    120
Bede, 31
Benson, Larry D., 27, 45, 46
Beowulf: oral-formulaic composition of,
    20, 23–24, 25, 109; analysis by
    formula, 41, 44–45, 88
Bible, oral theory of, 34
Bird of the Filial Return theme, 118–
    125
Boat motif, 110–112, 111, 113

Cicada-grasshopper motif, 8, 9
Ch'en Huan, 10
Cheng Hsüan, 2, 3, 5, 6, 37, 104, 105
Ch'i, house of, 69, 71, 95
Chou house poems, 48, 49, 50, See
    also *Sung* section
Chou, Rites of, 3, 71, 111
Chu Hsi, 9
Chu Tung-jun, 10
Compositional technique. *See* For-
    mula, Oral-formulaic poetry, Theme
Concatenate motif, 109, 110, 111, 113,
    117, 119, 120–121, 123
Confucius, on study of *Shih Ching*, 4, 6,
    64, 89, 108
Council theme, 21–22
Creed, Robert P., 25, 26, 44, 45, 46,
    99–100, 121
Crowne, David P., 19, 109
Culley, Robert, C., 34, 58, 59, 102
Cynewulf, 24, 26, 45, 46, 87, 127

Diamond, Robert E., 19, 26, 45, 46
Dobson, W. A. C. H., 36, 48–49; on
    stock phrases, 13, 14, 90–91

Enjambement, 38, 57
Epic poetry, 10, 88, 110

Ethical emphasis of *Shih Ching*, 3, 4
Exile theme, 19, 108

Feng element. See *Sung* element
Feng section, 36, 46, 47, 48–49, 50, 55,
    110
Flashing light motif, 109
Folk character of poetry, 69, 86
Form, elements of, 1, 2, 15, 33
Formative age, 95–96
Formula: definitions, 16, 17, 18, 26,
    35, 41–42, 43, 53; composition by,
    16, 25, 44–46, 47, 57, 58, 59, 62, 66,
    70, 87–88, 102, *see also* Gestalt
    preverbal level; uses of, 22, 41, 44–
    45, 98; flexibility of, 39–41, 52, 62,
    80; categories of, 41–42, 44–45, 50,
    51, 53, 54, 78, 103; expressions, 42,
    43, 50–52; statistical analysis, 43–50,
    55, 58, 59; length of, 43–44, 45, 46;
    clusters, 51–54, 66, 70–71, 79, 80,
    82, 87, 113, 115; system, 14, 18, 21,
    42, 88–90
Fry, Donald K., 25, 44, 53
Fu element. See *Hsing* element
Fu Szu-nien, 92–93, 94

Gestalt preverbal level, 22, 53, 56, 62,
    94
Great Preface, 1, 3
Greenfield, Stanley B., 16, 19, 79, 103,
    104n, 107

Hainsworth, J. B., 40–41, 47
Han age, 5, 21, 77, 106
Hero on the Beach theme, 19, 24, 109,
    110, 118
Historical criticism of *Shih Ching*, 5–14
Homeric poems, 17–18, 38, 100; for-
    mulaic aspects of, 15, 16, 22–23, 41,
    42, 43, 88
Hsaing, King, 77
Hsien-yün tribes, 29
Hsing element, 6, 12, 13, 77, 89, 101,
    102, 111–112, 117, 119, 121–122,
    127–128; definition, 3, 8, 9; verse,
    103, 106–107, 110
Hsüan, King, 77–78

DATE DUE

DEMCO 38-297